Y0-BUB-345

New Accents
in
Contemporary
Theology

New Accents
in
Contemporary
Theology

by Roger Hazelton

GREENWOOD PRESS, PUBLISHERS
WESTPORT, CONNECTICUT

Library of Congress Cataloging in Publication Data

Hazelton, Roger, 1909-
  New accents in contemporary theology.

  Reprint of the ed. published by Harper, New York.
  Bibliography: p.
  Includes index.
  1. Christianity--Philosophy. I. Title.
[BT40.H35 1979]   230   78-12237
ISBN 0-313-21181-7

Reprinted with the permission of Harper & Row, Publishers, Inc.

Reprinted in 1979 by Greenwood Press, Inc.,
51 Riverside Avenue, Westport, CT 06880

Printed in the United States of America

10 9 8 7 6 5 4 3 2 1

Contents

Foreword

Here are five brief chapters touching upon various themes and issues in contemporary Christian thinking. They are not offered as a rapid tour through theology-land. Instead they are intended as a series of explorations into different kinds of theological terrain, with a view toward whetting the reader's appetite for more intensive inquiry in these directions. What I hope to convey is something of the meaning of theology itself in terms of what are called here its new accents at the present time. Some of these accents represent reversals of the dominant trend of the last 30 or 40 years, especially in Europe. Others constitute a deepening and strengthening of long-continued emphases and concerns. But all of them are useful and important in affording glimpses into the nature of theological work, and that is why they are included here.

This will probably impress some readers as a highly subjective account of movements in contemporary theology; assuredly it is a selective, personal one. That is because my purpose is to invite participation in the theological task rather than to give a panorama of the theological scene. If such participation can be secured through this singling out of problems and sharing of enthusiasms, I shall be well content.

The book is based upon addresses given at Columbia University in the summer of 1958, expanded and reworked as the Swander Lectures at Lancaster Theological Seminary in November of the same year. I have also drawn upon articles published in *Theology and Life* and in the *Journal of Religious Thought*. I wish particularly to express my thanks to President Robert Moss and Professor Bela Vassady, my hosts at Lancaster, and to Mrs. Charles M. Leslie for assistance with the manuscript.

ROGER HAZELTON

Theology as Conversation: With the Arts

All noble art is devout.
—Michelangelo

I   It does us good sometimes to be reminded that Christian theology is a thoroughly human business. One of the surest signs of this is that theology, from first to last, is a kind of conversation. To some, it seems to be a very special sort of language called "divinity"; to others, it is merely the "darkening of counsel by words without knowledge." But either way, theology is obviously talk. It is carried on by means of talk, veritably bathed in talk, at times all but lost in talk.

Contrary to a widespread popular impression, theology is not solely a matter of propositions stated and positions taken. Perhaps it cannot better be defined than as a reasoning together about God. Hence nothing becomes a theologian like humility. One can scarcely speak habitually, and indeed professionally, about God without having to ask himself at frequent intervals whether he even has the right to do so, and how he may know that what he says is true. Such questions are both necessary and salutary to the enterprise of theology itself, and its integrity depends upon their being raised and met.

Realizing this, someone recently remarked in the midst of a

strenuous debate that theology is only a matter of "knocking a few heads together." To be sure, the reputation of theologians for contentiousness and pugnacity is so general that it cannot be wholly undeserved. If the theological air is thick with acrimony and arguments *ad hominem*, that may be because theology is not a series of set speeches but a way of thinking through and talking out together what is meant by God, man, sin, salvation, church, or Kingdom. The fact that it is always a learning from each other, a continuous corroborating and correcting, gives to contemporary theology in particular its special tone and color.

Disagreement is usually more interesting than agreement, and it may also be more significant. It is essential to the probing of issues which might otherwise be concealed by a premature politeness. The ultimate sort of questions with which theologians are grappling can hardly be resolved by rules of etiquette, and merely verbal harmony may only mask deep cleavages in Christian thought and life.

Yet there is real agreement, too, in today's theological enterprise. Schools of thought are formed which exhibit a remarkable amount of self-preservation. Certain strains of interest and of loyalty keep showing up throughout the centuries. Divergent modes of tradition and conviction possess a striking tenacity of form and content. Conversation presupposes some measure of real community, and this is clearly the case in contemporary Christian thinking. There is today a genuine theological community, in the same sense that there is a business community or an academic community, for example. Theologians are people who have developed their own ways of working, their own habits of thinking, and indeed their own language, made necessary by the central and controlling concern to which they are devoted.

This theological community is also, fortunately, an ecumenical community, as we shall see more clearly later on. By this I do not mean that denominational exclusiveness has been altogether overcome; on the contrary, its symptoms are still only too apparent. Yet it becomes increasingly plain today that all efforts to confine Christian truth in sectarian molds, whether Protestant or Catholic in character, are vestigial and anachronistic. Contemporary theology is by and large more ecumenical than are inherited practices in worship and patterns of organization within Christendom.

Despite its residue of denominational fixation and defensiveness, it has already proved itself to be capable of ecumenical flexibility and amplitude.

Think of theology, then, as a community of inquiry and conviction operating within and on behalf of the whole Church of Christ. It has a relationship to the Church not unlike that of a research laboratory to a great industry. Not that we in the churches pay our theologians to do our thinking for us, much less our believing. Theologians, nevertheless, are in a real sense set apart to do for the whole Church something that emphatically needs to be done, but which the Church in its every part and function cannot do. Theirs is primarily of course an intellectual task—that of understanding and making understandable the truth of Christian faith. Such a task, it is clear, must be shared by many disciplined workers who bring differing, yet finally complementary, perspectives to their common concern.

All this is involved in calling Christian theology a kind of conversation. In this chapter and the next, however, I shall be using the word "conversation" in a more special sense. In order to make plain its meaning I should like to venture a contrast between two sorts of movement in theology, two stresses, if you will, that together make up what might be called the theological rhythm. It is commonplace to remark that the assumptions of one generation often turn out to be the problems of the next. Historical generalizers have therefore been fond of employing the metaphor of the swing of a pendulum from one extreme to the other. Not long ago a visiting British lecturer even went so far as to compare the course of modern theology, rather inelegantly, to the zigzag motion of a drunken man lurching from side to side!

A much more helpful and revealing image for understanding theological development is one borrowed from physiology—the rhythms of systole and diastole in the human heart. As the heart does its work in the body by alternately expanding and contracting, opening and closing, so does theology work within the body of Christ called the Church. There are times when Christian faith has to turn inward upon itself, asking what is authentically and ultimately its own kind of truth. Then theology becomes an essay in self-discovery and self-definition. At other times it becomes imperative for theologians to move out into the world again, on the basis of this self-understanding, seeking out and coming to grips with those modes of truth from which earlier they had strategically withdrawn. Then theology enters upon a phase of exploration and engagement; to borrow the words of Robert Frost, it has "a lover's quarrel with the world."

We are now shifting from the first of these phases, which has dominated the so-called "neo-orthodoxy" of the recent past, into the second phase, which is an attempt to get back into theological touch with the world, to resume conversations which in some cases have been broken off for several centuries. Theology today and tomorrow has for one of its major purposes the rediscovery and repossession, in Christ's name, of vast territories of human culture which have long been lost to the Christian intelligence.

This purpose informs each of the new accents and approaches in theology which we shall sketch and appraise in the following chapters. But it particularly illuminates the concept of theology as conversation with which we are now concerned. Those who are taking part in the newer phase are no less eager than their immediate predecessors to speak the truth disclosed in Christian faith; but they are at the same time more ready to *listen* to truth coming from other quarters formerly called "secular." The very word "secular," in fact, is at present being attacked on definitely theological and Christian grounds. The line between sacred and secular, between holy and profane, is no longer as sharp or plain as it once seemed to be. The reasons for this situation are not wholly those of cultural change itself, but some at least proceed from the Christian faith's own understanding of itself as world-responsible and world-redeeming.

Living within the circle of faith does not mean being closed away from or being set against the world so much as being confronted by and open to the world. It involves the most drastic sort of exposure to unwelcome experience and unfamiliar truth. It finds charity and hope to be not simply moral but also intellectual virtues. Not only does it see in every unbeliever a neighbor for whom Christ died, but even in physical nature it finds disclosed the glory and the grandeur that is God's.

The stirring of this newer movement within contemporary thought means that the entire concept of theology as giving answers to the world's questions, or as fitting the Christian message systematically into the human situation, is itself being called into question. While we do not deny that theology always consists of the response of our minds to God's own Word spoken in Jesus Christ, we find it very difficult to think that God has given us exclusive charge over this Word or that we come to possess it through any kind of privileged communication. Precisely by learning to listen more attentively in faith to God as he speaks to us, we have been brought to listen more eagerly and willingly to those who speak from outside our self-drawn theological circle. We can now hear disturbing reverberations of the Word made flesh in some of the most unlikely voices raised in our day. Tertullian's ancient question, "What has Athens to do with Jerusalem?" no longer seems so purely rhetorical. We are more inclined to answer, using the words of St. Paul, "Much, every way."

Already the theological conversation with these voices has begun. In this chapter and the next we shall be overhearing three such conversations going on right now between Christian theologians and those who are working chiefly in the arts, the sciences, and philosophy. In each case a degree of genuine communication has opened up which is steadily growing. Old reticences and recriminations are being overcome. Gulfs of suspicion and hostility, lately thought to be impassable, are being slowly bridged. A frank interchange of difficulties and aims, of doubts and enthusiasms, is under way.

It must be admitted that there are still numerous barriers to be thrown down, and bridges to be crossed, in each of these preliminary conversations. Hence we may expect, for some time to come, verbal skirmishing and ideological maneuvering as the participants get acquainted, feel one another out, learn patience and mutual respect. What is most significant, however, is that these conversations are taking place at all. My purpose here is only to convey something of their substance and their spirit, in the hope that the reader may be encouraged to enter upon one or more of them himself.

II   One of the most noteworthy facts about contemporary theology is the new interest that theologians everywhere are taking in the various art forms, as well as in critical and esthetic theory.

To one who has been brought up theologically on Barth and Brunner, Niebuhr and Nygren, it is startling, to say the least, to find one's fellow theologians reading Baudelaire or Rilke, listening to off-beat music and going to off-Broadway shows. This kind of willing exposure, however, is the price that has to be paid for the rewinning of those lost provinces of culture, a task which now has a high theological priority among us. It was a French Protestant lay theologian, Denis de Rougemont, who provided a sort of charter for this movement more than a decade ago. "All the culture of the West," he wrote, "—music, painting, philosophy, literature—came out of the churches and the convents, but, alas, it also went out of them! It is time that we struggle to find it again and bring it back."[1]

In this struggle some of us have been learning things we never should have forgotten—for example, that a novel by someone who, like Faulkner or Camus, does not wish to be known as a Christian believer may come closer to the biblical and churchly truth about man than a Sunday morning sermon; that a pair of old shoes painted by van Gogh may be far more meaningful religiously than a head of Jesus by Sallman or Hofmann; and that the artist's way of life, in its strictness and dedication, has astonishingly much in common with that of the Christian saint.

This new theological interest has many causes and motives, but as yet it lacks a rationale. The conversation with the arts is still in its early stages. Yet it is by no means a one-sided theological effort, as numerous conferences, exhibitions, and other experiments in collaboration testify. It is a welcome fact that creative artists no longer go out of their way to avoid the traditional symbols and emphases of Christianity. However, the *rapprochement* is still far from being an *entente cordiale*. Recently a group of painters, at a conference with theologians in Switzerland, expressed quite openly their feeling of isolation from the Church, complaining that Christians are generally not interested in what art has to contribute to their faith and life. And in theology, there are lingering traces of the old suspicion and embarrassment in the presence of the arts. Back in the beginning of the nineteenth century Schleiermacher wrote his celebrated essays "to the

[1] "The Christian Opportunity," in *The Third Hour*, New York, Issue III, 1947.

cultured despisers of Christianity." Today, in the middle of the
twentieth, there are those who write and speak as if they were
the Christian despisers of culture.

Nevertheless, there is at present a healthier situation of willing
exposure and robust encounter *vis-à-vis* the arts than most of us,
especially those in Protestant churches, have ever known before.
On each side of the conversation there is growing readiness and
even eagerness to learn the other's language. This is of course
where any deeper understanding must begin.

At first, theologians used the arts primarily as symptoms or
indexes of the state of contemporary culture—that is, as documentation for a theological analysis and critique of human self-
sufficiency and estrangement from God. Paul Tillich's early writings, especially *The Religious Situation*, give a telling illustration
of this sort of interest in the arts. His analyses of the poetry of
Rilke or the painting of Schmidt-Rottluff proceed on the very
true assumption that art reveals the character of man's spiritual
situation and is therefore indispensable to the theologian.

The second stage, on which some of us believe ourselves to be
already standing, is less assured theologically while at the same
time more of a genuine dialogue with the art forms of the present.
It keeps up a running conversation on fairly specific issues, such
as the nature of the tragic, the comparison of Christian with
classical styles of writing, the meaning of word, image, or myth,
the idea of a Christian poetics or esthetics in reaction against the
"new Aristotelianism" of some present-day critics, and the relationships between imagination and belief. This second level is
more flexible and tentative in character than the first. It has
chiefly to do with the mutual bearings of art and faith, and so of
esthetics and theology, upon one another.

In some respects this stage is more difficult than the first, since
it makes more and harder demands upon the parties to the conversation. It is always easier to use the arts for hortatory, polemical,
or systematic purposes than to seek a communicable ground with
theory and criticism. This is in part because esthetics, like modern
art itself, has been rapidly developing in an autonomous and even
anti-theological direction. For as the fabric of the Christian vision
of the world was broken, the various disciplines and endeavors of
men lost their religious anchorage and began to seem self-explain-

ing and self-justifying. Nowhere was this more true than in the case of modern art. Yet esthetics, although equally autonomous, did not take exactly the same course as did the arts. It remained an essentially philosophical discipline, reflecting not so much the preoccupations and intentions of artists themselves as those of various positions within metaphysics, epistemology, or logic. Esthetics, speaking generally, has not been expressionist or impressionist, imagist or realist, cubist or surrealist in its orientation; it has been instead Marxist, naturalist, idealist, pragmatist, or phenomenological.

Another part of the difficulty lies in the fact that both theology and esthetics represent types of reflective inquiry rather than elemental human interests. Theology is to religious faith as esthetics is to art. That is, both constitute a critical and sustained effort to comprehend and state the structures of meaning, or intelligible relations, which underlie these two more basic human activities. Hence there is not only a deep cleavage between art and faith, lasting almost four centuries, with its freight of isolation and suspicion, to be overcome. There are also the internal tensions between artist and critic, as between believer and thinker, to be resolved. These tensions sometimes occur within a single person, in which case they may prove unbearably acute and destructive. In a few instances, on the other hand, they have become fruitful and creative.

Granting these problems, what is the possibility of a theological esthetics in our day? Let us see just what this phrase can mean. At first glance it would seem to indicate something like the bridge sciences such as biochemistry or astrophysics. We would then be putting our attention upon a supposedly common zone to which both theological and esthetic categories and methods might be said to apply. Let us take an example from what is customarily called "sacred" art. A painting of the crucifixion obviously falls within both perspectives. That is, it has to be judged not only as to its artistic genuineness but also as to its Christian rightness. The latter criterion has to do with questions such as these: Does the Christ figure portrayed stand in positive and recognizable relation to the Christ of the Bible and the creeds? Is the event depicted congruous in its meaning and effect with that which stands at the center of the Christian faith? Does the emphasis fall upon a struggle to the death between God and the powers of darkness, or does a sentimental and pathetic humanism crowd out all thought of the mysterious and the transcendent? A theologian would want these questions answered in the affirmative, and he has every right to ask them of a work which is called a crucifixion.

A complete and relevant account of such a work should include both kinds of judgment, and ideally they should be combined within the same interpreter or critic. But this combination, however desirable, is very rarely found. Most of us do well to settle for collaboration with someone who is able to supply our own deficiencies, as Sir Herbert Read makes use of Collingwood or as Maritain depends on Jean Cocteau and Georges Rouault. As matters now stand, this meaning of the phrase "theological esthetics" rightly points to the need for joint effort by theologians and interpreters of art; it can hardly mean an articulate discipline capable at once of determining both artistic excellence and Christian adequacy.

So let us try a second tack. The phrase might mean, "theology of the esthetic experience." So understood, it would be comparable to certain branches of philosophy like the philosophy of politics, history, or science. It would seek to give the *raison d'être* of the making and meaning of works of art. Its field would be as broad as art itself, not restricted to sacred or religious art. In short, it would be esthetics over again but with theological interests predominating. This would be quite in line with Paul Tillich's view that art is implicitly religious, or has "ultimate concern," because it is the instrument by which man wrestles with the full and deep reality of his situation in the world.

The second way of rendering "theological esthetics" has at least two striking difficulties. One is the over-intellectualizing of the forms of art, the bending and twisting of what is there to suit one's own schematic purposes. This happens, for example, when Erwin Panofsky tries to understand Gothic art as the projection of scholastic philosophy. His brilliant *tour de force* shows how the theological and philosophical format of medieval logic can become too controlling. It is easy to forget that the twin towers of Notre Dame had risen long before St. Thomas Aquinas began writing his *Summa Theologica*. In fact, art forms are among the first,

and not the last, signs of a changed human consciousness of ultimate reality.

A further difficulty arises from the misunderstanding of theology
itself which such a view of theological esthetics may promote.
When we speak of the "theology of culture" or the "theology
of history" we may be making claims for theology which cannot
be made good. There is something decidedly presumptuous in the
implication that theology is a sort of master perspective by which
any sort of event or meaning can be reckoned with and put in its
proper intellectual place.

Perhaps this difficulty comes from a confusion between theology
and philosophy. Those like Gustav Aulén who wish to dissociate
theology completely from philosophy often end by regarding
theology as a kind of super-philosophy. It is as if they were saying
that theology does not need philosophical support or criticism
because it contains within itself all the values which philosophy
might otherwise provide. Many so-called "neo-orthodox" theologians today are quite abrupt in their dismissal of philosophy from
the perspective of theology; but they are seldom aware that this
involves making philosophical claims for theology itself.

Our view in this book is a very different one. Theology is related
to philosophy, including esthetics, not as a substitute but as a
corrective. It is true that it shares with all philosophy its synoptic,
comprehensive aim and character. But it cannot displace philosophy, either as a whole or in any of its branches. So, for example,
theological ethics is certainly more than philosophical ethics, but
it is still ethics and therefore also philosophical. The only alternative would seem to be that of saying that theological ethics is
not even ethical. Why should it be otherwise with theological
esthetics?

This bring up a third possibility. Why not speak of theological
esthetics as theology controlled by esthetic considerations? In
effect this changes the phrase to read "esthetic theology." The
possibility is not unattractive, and it has actually been tried,
notably by Jonathan Edwards in his *Treatise on the Religious
Affections* and *The Nature of True Virtue*. This at any rate pre-
serves the integrity of esthetic experience and its values, regarding
it as in some sense revelatory of what is divine or sacred. It takes
seriously the beauty of holiness by converting it into the holiness

of beauty. So what moral theology did for morality, or natural theology did for the natural sciences, esthetic theology might then do for art.

This course has much to commend it, since it effectively counteracts the proud isolation of a great deal of contemporary theology, especially its pretensions to be omni-relevant and omni-categorical. Yet it does leave some things to be desired. While any sector of human interest or endeavor may indeed lead one ultimately to think in terms of God, it does not follow that this is true of such an interest or endeavor taken simply as it stands and speaking only for itself. Although any subject may have dimensions that are ultimately theological, these are not necessarily intrinsic or inherent in it. They have to be pointed out, and even then they are not always granted by those who ought to know. This, then, suggests that dimensions of theological meaning and relevance are brought to bear upon the subject, instead of being developed solely from within it. A theology which would be no more than an extension or magnification of esthetics is simply a contradiction in terms.

III   Where does all this leave us with the phrase we have been considering? I would still defend its use on three important grounds. First, "theological esthetics" suggests rightly that theology is fundamental to esthetic understanding. There may still be some sense in which theology can be made out to be the queen of the sciences; I think we are on more solid ground if we regard it as their maidservant. Speaking less metaphorically, theology does provide principles of meaning which are indispensable to the full elucidation of any object or situation, but this is not the same as saying that theological principles are *central* to such elucidation. The distinction between what is central and what is fundamental for our thought is very often slurred; it has, however, signal importance for one's outlook and method in any field.

An illustration comes readily to mind from the realm of esthetics. The words "creation" and "creative" are frequently invoked to describe a quality of artistic effort and imagination. Clearly, these are theological terms which have been borrowed and transferred, perhaps unconsciously, often by thinkers who deny the reference of such words to any ground of being beyond the artist's self. True, this secularizing of theological language has often taken place before, and it can hardly be prevented now. Yet if artistic creativity is going to be understood in an explicitly Christian fashion, certain convictions of faith become at once pertinent—the creation of the world by God, the affirmation of that created world as therefore good, and man's God-given capacity to be creative in his own turn and sphere. Although our center of attention is still upon the artist and his work and its effect, this esthetic delineation proceeds from a theological base which indeed is indispensable to its development.

In the second place, theology itself needs to be seen in the light of esthetics. This point we must work out at somewhat greater length, as it involves the whole vexed question of symbols and symbolism. After all, we theologians are fellow workers with the artists. Ours also is the task of conveying the mystery of the real. We are engaged in symbolizing the fact that, as Nicolas Berdyaev said, God is the meaning of human existence. We work in patterns of words, which are tokens of a reality they body forth but cannot contain; and our purpose is not merely to expound or instruct, but to persuade and convince. This makes theology itself an art—the art of rhetoric—which ought to be judged as such by frankly esthetic standards. There is an intimate but seldom-seen connection between a person's thought and his style, which Alfred North Whitehead defined precisely as "the ultimate morality of mind."

Let us pause here long enough to say that the disciplined shaping of thought into speech is itself part of theology, despite the fact that much theological writing is very bad writing indeed. How did the notion ever get abroad that rigorous thinking and fine writing are at loggerheads with each other? Is it not a Christian insight that truth is a manner, as well as a matter, of saying or of living? One hopes for the time when theological writing will be not only more lucid but also more congruous in form with the bodying-forth in Christ of God's own speech to mankind, that is, more truly symbolic of the divine.

Theology always understands itself better if it is alert to its own esthetic involvements and intentions, and obviously it understands the arts better as well. Søren Kierkegaard may be a case in point.

He was far more of an esthetician, and certainly more of an artist, than he ever seemed willing to admit. His entire contribution to modern theology is marked by a rhetorical brilliance, a precise use of literary paradox, and a carefully wrought stylistic rapport with the reader which are all too seldom recognized. The great Augustine also was singularly able to bring speech and thought together, each to the service of the other, in luminous and eloquent utterance. His own considerable experience as a teacher of rhetoric, as well as his schooling in biblical literature, accounts in part for his gift; but it is due even more to the fact that in himself, and therefore also in his style, he had fused classical and Christian perspectives, modes of feeling, insights. Although this fusion is widely regarded by scholars as a liability, it actually gave St. Augustine a great advantage in theological communication: and it still does.

Third, theological esthetics includes the idea which Brother George Every, Geddes MacGregor, and others have been calling "Christian discrimination." It is unfortunate that this phrase should bring to mind primarily church censorship, as expressed in the "Legion of Decency" campaign waged by the Roman Catholic hierarchy. Christian bodies have a lot of lost ground to recover before they can set themselves up as keepers of the public conscience in the matter of the arts. To be sure, gross offenses against common decency, if and when they occur in the mass media, should be exposed and condemned; but here ridicule is apt to be a better weapon than reprisal. Attempts at church censorship lack nothing so much as humor; they tend to treat films, plays, or books not as works of art but in narrowly moral fashion; and their worst result is found in the inoffensive mediocrity of the majority of works offered in the popular market. Our conversation with the arts must go much farther before we can act wisely and effectively in this direction.

Meanwhile, however, there are movies, plays, books, concerts, and exhibitions to be reviewed. This can and should be done with motives and standards that are demonstrably Christian. The Protestant newspaper *La Réforme* has already been doing this for years in Paris; in our own country *The Christian Century* is now regularly reviewing Broadway productions, which is all to the good. But much more might be done along the same line, especially since painters and playwrights no longer shy away from religious implications as they formerly did. It is always disappointing to see how competent and respected drama critics simply draw a blank when Christian themes or images are brought upon the stage. They seem baffled and inept when confronting them. And so they miss the whole point of an author's or an actor's work, indulging instead in merely preferential or pontificating judgments that betray their own ignorance of the Christian heritage and vision. It is even more dismaying when such lack of Christian discrimination is in evidence within the very worship of the churches with respect to the liturgical arts; but it is less excusable.

This sort of discrimination, it may be argued, is the province of criticism rather than esthetics. The answer is that, while this is clearly so, any valid theory of art must show itself capable of judging works of art. Esthetics is expressed in criticism, just as it is implied in criticism. Christian discrimination is not all that theological esthetics means, but it is plainly included in that meaning. For criticism is not a no man's land subsisting somewhere between art and the theory of art. As Theodore Greene has well reminded and shown us in his book *The Arts and the Art of Criticism*, criticism is itself both an art and the theory of art. Hence it is an especially crucial instance of what theological esthetics might be said to mean.

Christian criticism is naturally most needful in those cases where Christian subject matter or convictions are being treated in the arts. Here an artist exposes himself to theological conversation whether he likes it or not. But it is not the artist's so-called "theology" which the Christian critic has to put to the test, but the congruity or fitness of his work as it is measured by both historic and contemporary Christian experience. It is not, at least initially, a question of the artist's "orthodoxy"; it is a matter of his fidelity to the Christian ordering of things, which is, after all, marked by a certain consistency and displays a rather unlooked-for degree of consensus on some major points. In the task of Christian discrimination, then, theology may serve more as a reminder than as a rule.

Any work of art is both expressive and impressive and so must be reckoned with on both counts. This, I believe, is where Paul Tillich's view of the relation between religion and art sadly fails us. He does not provide us with anything like a perspective for Christian discrimination because he thinks of the art work as wholly expressive and judges it accordingly. His conception of a "religious style" comes remarkably close to that of German expressionism, as John Dixon and others have noticed.[2] The work of art is for Tillich an ontological tool or token; it is not, however, a seal or pledge of reality in the Christian, sacramental sense.

But if I read Pascal's "Mystery of Jesus" or see El Greco's "Agony in the Garden," something more than merely expressive communication is taking place. There is also a mode of impressive communication in these works which I do not hesitate to call evangelical. This, if you like, is the "message" in all religious art; not something which can be extracted from them and set down in propositions for one's approval or rejection in Christian terms, but the Word made flesh, the speech of God to men about himself.

IV   Let us focus on one matter which has been very prominent in the conversation between theology and the arts, that of symbols and symbolism. This matter greatly needs clarification in an age like ours "obsessed with technique, hagridden by Facts, in love with information"[3]—an age in which a condescending scientism remains in vogue despite the valiant efforts of scientists themselves to counteract it. True science gives no license to an attitude which refuses the right of any other kind of symbolism than science itself to report and communicate truth. The highly technical symbols of the scientist are not basically different, as such, from those symbols native to the artist or the believer. Symbolism of whatever sort is man's way of protesting against the "mereness" of his experience; almost by definition, it is the denial of sheer, unstructured "thinginess" or bare factuality. Symbols are the way in which we recast the stuff of human experience—here we have to use this large, amorphous word—in self-fulfilling, self-enlarging terms. This is as true of an algebraic equation or chemical formula as when the symbol happens to be an angel, moonlight, or the Holy Spirit.

---

[2] See Dixon's article "On the Possibility of a Christian Criticism of the Arts," in *The Christian Scholar*, December, 1957.

[3] Dwight Macdonald, "The Triumph of the Fact," in *The Anchor Review* (New York: Doubleday, 1957), p. 113.

The same point may be made the other way around. A symbol not only extends and so enriches our experience, but also condenses and embodies it in concretely meaningful pattern or form: our experience is always greater than our knowledge, sensibility outruns sensation, our reach exceeds our grasp. The aim of symbolism is to match this disproportion by some built-in capacity for recognizing and representing it. "Contracting the immensities," John Donne called it; and Shakespeare said the same thing in more familiar words:

> And, as imagination bodies forth
> The forms of things unknown, the poet's pen
> Turns them to shapes, and gives to airy nothing
> A local habitation and a name.

A symbol is just this shaping, naming, bodying-forth of what would otherwise remain shapeless, nameless, fugitive; and even one's definition of the symbol must, like Donne's or Shakespeare's, be itself symbolic through and through.

This is axiomatic in the arts but it should be more often and more generously admitted in theology. The great ecumenical creeds were known in the early church as "symbols" of faith and their study by theologians has until quite recently been called "symbolics." Their avowed purpose was to state what is unstatable, that is, to use language to shape and name a saving, sovereign truth. The creed says what Christians mean, to be sure; but it also means more than they can possibly say, and this too it somehow manages to say. Its propositions are, at bottom, pictures— numinous, charged with symbolic potency and suggestiveness; it is a work of art in spite of itself.

Our Christian faith is never communicated except by means of symbols. And the symbols are not simply figures and pictures in colored glass or wood or stone but the central affirmations and actions by which we body forth our faith. We live inevitably by word and gesture, song and story, for we are intent upon contracting the immensities, upon conveying things invisible through things visible.

This of course can easily be misunderstood, leading the weak-minded into a false and overblown estheticism which is as far from the truth about Christian symbols as is a stubborn literalism.

We may charm ourselves into church, be lulled into purring acceptance of familiar symbols for their own sweet sakes, and acquire a kind of "cathedral complex." According to Sir Herbert Read, something like this happened in Christian art toward the close of the medieval period when an elaborate and mannered manipulation of symbols all but destroyed the vital communication of what Read calls "the miracle of pure Being." In many quarters the same sort of thing is happening today.

But it does not have to happen. One of the guarantees against its happening is the principle that our symbols can be taken seriously only if they are *not* taken literally. We use them to get at the truth only if we regard them as not confining the truth. For how can you take a symbol literally, when even letters are symbols? The opposite of literalness is not playfulness but truthfulness—that truthful consciousness which, as Collingwood and Read have told us, is the foundation of all authentic art.

This principle for making and using symbols becomes doubly important if the inherited symbolism of our faith is to find any common ground with those new symbols by which artists at the present time seek to body forth the meaning—or, it may be, the meaninglessness—of man's life upon the earth. The cross, to take perhaps the most significant example, is not merely a pointer to a place in history where we believe something of ultimate importance happened, although it is also that. The cross is a symbol making plain what theologians now are beginning to call the *cruciform nature of human existence* itself: the fulfilling of life is found only on the other side of losing life.

Indeed, the meaning of the cross to Christian faith may throw real light upon the nature of symbolism itself. The most effective symbol for conveying the mystery of what is real is the symbol which conveys its own inadequacy along with what is bodied forth. The symbol, that is, has a built-in reserve or hesitation before the mystery of the real, a kind of wonder and even limp before that which cannot be fully voiced or pictured. This, I believe, is what Professor Tillich has been emphasizing when he speaks of the necessity for a "broken myth" and a "broken symbol" in religious art. The difference between the sort of symbol which is merely a counter or unit of exchange in human communication and that which shares in the very reality it symbolizes lies just here. The latter symbol must be broken in order to convey; it must be kept from calling exclusive attention to itself, that it may both express and impress the reality it carries. Success in and because of failure, triumph precisely through tragedy, God in the form of man—these meanings can come through to us only in this broken way. All the symbols of theology or of Christian art that really matter are broken symbols. They deliberately limp and hesitate in the presence of what they mean to say. Once fashioned, they are purposely broken so that they may not become substitutes for what gives them their reason for meaning and for being.

"Art and religion at their best," writes Samuel H. Miller, "seek to get at the fundamental reality of life by stripping it of its superficial aspects. . . . They both work in images, by the endless and patient exercise of the imagination, delving beneath the surface of the customary and taken-for-granted, encountering the immediate and original mysteries of beauty and holiness." The point is abundantly confirmed by artists themselves—for example, by Robert Frost, who says that what art does for life is to shape it, to strip it to form, or by Georges Rouault, who declares that in painting the essential thing is to strip oneself.

These affirmations should be taken very much in earnest if we are going to understand, much less appreciate, the intent and achievement of contemporary art. Probably we shall have with us for some time to come the picture-postcard painting of the plush galleries and what is often termed the "Sunday school art" of most of our churches. But the authentic work of the present is not commodity or market art; it has instead the truthful, exposed, even ruthless quality of a style which wants nothing so much as to say just how and where man really lives. Thus it challenges all sentimental, moralizing literalism, whether Catholic or Protestant, by an image of reality which may well be more profoundly Christian than is our Christianity itself.

"An image of reality"—but is not reality the precise opposite of images and imagining? There is certainly within our own religious heritage a long record of disapproval and rejection where the human imagination is involved. All this will need to be overcome if the conversation between theologians and artists on issues connected with symbolism is to flourish and bear fruit. But the task will not be easy. Human imagination has been long suspect in Christian circles. Some have applied to it the words of Paul, "Be not wise in your own conceits"; the mystic St. Theresa called it "the fool in the house," that is, disorderly and untidying factor in the human spirit; and Blaise Pascal considered it to be "the deceiving part of man."

Since the interpretation of symbol and image presented here is quite in contrast to this traditional one, it will repay us to sketch it in fairly clear outline. Undoubtedly the imagination does create problems for Christian faith, but not the sort of problems created by a disturbing and distorting element in an otherwise reality-centered human person. This can be seen if we look deeper, listening to artists themselves as they describe their own aim and task. Here is Picasso saying, "Art is a lie that makes us realize the truth." Could there be a more exact, if paradoxical, statement of the matter? In this respect, art and religion are at one. The symbolizing, or imaging, which goes on in both has its origin in man's desire, not to flee reality, or even to transform it, but to gain a firmer hold on reality. In both art and faith there occurs that searching after what is real which has already been termed the stripping-down of life; and in that search, the human imagination is by no means an intruder but a most necessary instrument and channel.

The man of art and the man of faith alike are marked by the knowledge that the real lies somewhere under the surfaces of things, as also by the single-mindedness and concentration required in order to reach and grasp the real. Between Francis of Assisi and Vincent van Gogh, for instance, there is simply not the distance of spirit which is all too frequently assumed to exist. Although St. Paul has been called "a writer who does not want to be such," he was quite aware that faith in Jesus Christ has its own proper rhetoric. As Amos Wilder has noticed, he was not above adapting for his own missionary purposes the current counters of pagan esthetics: "Whatsoever is lovely, whatsoever is gracious, if there is any excellence, if there is any praise, think about these things."

This stress, however unwelcome to biblicists and purists, must be made today because of the repeated iconoclasm from which the entire Jewish-Christian tradition has sadly suffered. The eighth-century prophets, of course, were quite right to be vigorously exercised about idol worship, since this was naturally a great danger in a community with so meager a sense for plastic representation. If the Hebrew people had been as adept and knowing in their use of nonverbal, as well as verbal, symbols for communicating faith, they might have better grasped the true import and purpose of all symbolic forms. But since hearing, not seeing, was the characteristic mode of God's self-disclosure to them, oral instruction rather than visual symbolism became dominant. This made it difficult for them to discriminate between an image and an idol.

The same strain continued into the Christian era. Catacomb paintings were not so much artistic symbols as a kind of secret code or sign language. A historian has termed them "not art, but the mortification of art." The fathers of the church, for the most part, carried on this anti-esthetic viewpoint; certainly they did not know or care that they were producing "literature," and some, like Origen, even hesitated to write at all. Reasons both good and bad went into this Christian "fasting from art," not only in the early centuries but in the Reformation, when organ smashing and window breaking were done in the name of the Protestant's God.

Doubtless prophetic warnings such as First Isaiah's scathing denunciation of idolatry will always be needed in the churches, especially in view of our traditional ineptitude in handling religious symbols. They may be even more to the point in our own time, marked as it is by what Berdyaev called a bourgeois interest in appearance rather than in being. But is there not another voice which needs for more to be heard at the present moment? An image is not necessarily an idol although it may be in constant danger of turning into one. What is instrumental to our faith does not have to become a shoddy substitute for faith. In Christianity, at any rate, there is a sacramental premise alongside the prophetic premise. No symbol can possibly house God; that we know and must declare. Yet all things can reflect God's glory and announce his grace, precisely because they are his own creation. A name or a shape in this visible world can body forth, however brokenly, the invisible Lord of the world. Indeed, the Christian symbol must be made before it can be broken, and the breaking must be a part of its making.

If this created world is originally and finally God's world—and our faith states that it is—must it not give undeniable tokens of this truth? Art and the Christian faith stand basically together on both the prophetic and the sacramental premise. It is not a question of which is inherently the more essential or important, as they forever need each other and demand each other. At the present juncture, however, it should be said that the prophetic premise cannot be true unless the sacramental premise is also true. Perhaps Archbishop William Temple had this truth in mind when writing that worship is too spiritual a process to be able to dispense with the material; his statement, obviously, cuts both ways and applies to other Christian matters than liturgy and ritual.

Or we may say the same thing basically in the words of Peter Taylor Forsyth:

> The Christian mind is the reconciliation of Jew and Greek. . . . It reconciled the immanence and the eminence of God. . . . It has uplifted our thought together of the Creator and the work. . . . Man by redemption became free *from* the world *for* the world.[4]

This position, though highly unpopular in some Christian quarters, is nonetheless both historically just and theologically correct. What is more, it gives us a positive point of contact for continuing the Christian conversation with the contemporary arts.

V Art and faith alike, we have said, are engaged in a search for reality, the "lived reality" of which Ortega y Gasset writes so eloquently. Both artist and believer know well that things are not as they seem, and wish to initiate us into that same knowledge. To faith and art, the reality of life is at the same time the mystery of life. For what is more mysterious than the really real? And what is more real than the undeniably mysterious? This is why art and religion work within "the firmament of symbol"; how else could they do what they have to do, convey the mystery of the real? They both live at the frontier between sense and spirit which, as Coventry Patmore observed, is "the devil's hunting-ground"; and yet the same frontier is also where, if anywhere, the true God may be met and known.

To an artist like Georges Rouault, for whom religion was the central energy of his experience, painting becomes liturgical and

[4] In *Christ on Parnassus* (London: Hodder & Stoughton), pp. 82, 86.

evangelical, analogous in many respects to the poetry of Charles Péguy. Rouault's purpose is not so much portrayal as it is conveyance, not so much completeness as penetration. His works in color, says a recent poem in his honor, are "like enamelled Gothic reliquaries, with sombre rubies and shadowy sapphires, with a bit of silver such as one sees in dewy gardens." And his graphics, like the famous Miserere series, seem dominated by the figure of the Christ—Pascal's Christ, who will be in agony until the end of the world, the Christ of Grünewald and of Thomas à Kempis. In this kind of art we catch undoubted glimpses of a reality that is inexhaustibly mysterious, of a mystery that is infinitely real.

Clearly, in the case of Rouault, we have come very far from what is customarily termed "religious" art. Work such as his does not inform or instruct primarily; it may not even edify or in the usual sense inspire; but it does bear witness to the revealing, redeeming God. This witnessing character is the chief characteristic of all truly Christian art. By pointing both beyond and through itself, it testifies, gives evidence of things not seen, and so is man's way of keeping faith with what is eternal and divine. Its images and symbols have power in them to compose and perhaps also to change human life.

But there is both a positive and a negative kind of religious witness in contemporary art. The negative is the more familiar, as in Samuel Beckett's *Waiting for Godot* or Albert Camus's *The Fall*, in which we are shown God's absence and silence. Such works of art raise theological issues which may well make God appear more real as an object of radical doubt than he can ever be as the object of so-called faith. At least these works succeed in avoiding the downright blasphemy which lurks within our conventional churchly piety, the terrible profanity involved in taking God too much for granted.

The current conversation between theology and the arts has disclosed in an unparalleled way how relevant doubt and faith are for each other. It has shown that there is no convenient, comprehensive way of dividing the secular from the sacred. Hence it has enabled those of us who are willing to be known as Christian believers to identify ourselves imaginatively with the modern men and women whose lives are haunted by the silent, absent God. Theology as conversation is mightily interested in how doubt can be so strong where there is no avowed faith, since the deepest doubt always occurs when faith is most alive, as in the Book of Job.

Positive witness, on the other hand, is the artist's or the theologian's way of testifying from within faith and on faith's behalf. We may best conceive it as reconstituting the accepted symbols by bringing them into living connection with the negative symbols, which have given proof of their power to speak to the human condition in our time. This massive search for images which can body forth old truth in new shapes and names, and find new truth in classically Christian tokens, is already in full swing in architecture, drama, painting, music, and sculpture. The keynote of such positive witness is that of rediscovery and celebration, as the central facts of Christian existence are set forth again, but with how many surprises and with what fresh shocks of recognition!

Such witnessing as this is by no means merely a matter of content; it is one of style as well. The positive religious symbol channels what it communicates and is itself a fair sample of what it bodies forth. The fashionable word for such a process today is "icon," a word which plainly is borrowed from the Christian heritage. Rouault himself has gone to great lengths to give his paintings an icon-like quality, as when he splatters and flagellates the very surface of the material on which he draws the semblance of the scourged and stricken Savior.

The New Testament word which is applicable to the positive symbol is "earnest" or "pledge." Like the prophecies or parables of Scripture, the icon has both judgment and mercy in it, since it witnesses not only to a present claim but also to a future possibility. This feature of the biblical style has been compared to a down payment or a promissory note. The icon participates in the reality which it symbolizes, and this participation is not so much a question of subject as of style; for it is not as if we knew apart from symbol what was being symbolized. Hence symbols should not be handled arbitrarily or cavalierly, either as literal transcripts or as idea suggesters. They have, on Christian terms, their own mode of being or kind of reality which is decisive just because it is derivative.

Earlier we spoke of the way in which esthetic considerations may throw light upon the theologian's work; now perhaps we can see how theological truth may serve to illumine what goes on within the arts. In his essay on poetry and the poetic process called "The Dyer's Hand" W. H. Auden has written:

> Every poet, consciously or unconsciously, holds the following absolute presuppositions as the dogmas of his art:
>
> (1) A historical world of unique events and persons exists and its existence is a good.
>
> (2) This historical world is a fallen world, full of unfreedom and disorder. It is good that it exists but the way in which it exists is evil.
>
> (3) The historical world is a redeemable world. The unfreedom and disorder of the past can be reconciled in the future. Every successful poem, therefore, presents an analogue of that paradisal state in which Freedom and Law, System and Order are united, and contradictions reconciled and sins forgiven.[5]

These "dogmas" are strikingly parallel to what Santayana has called the Christian epic. Not all artists will agree, of course, that these are their working assumptions, but they might be willing to allow that art may be Christianly understood. Certainly theologians have at all events the right to put forward such categories and to test them out upon the various forms of contemporary art. In this way the conversation now begun may deepen and flourish. And it will not be confined to the discussion of works carrying the signature of religious commitment and concern, but will endeavor to make plain the meaning of all art in terms of its Christian significance.

Our warrant for doing this as theologians is simply that a work of art is a "word made flesh." As Eric Gill has said: "A word; that which emanates from mind. Made flesh; a thing seen, a thing known, the immeasurable translated into terms of the measurable. From the highest to the lowest that is the substance of works of art."[6] A theologian may aspire to think God's thoughts after him; an artist by the power of creative imagination is enabled to do God's work after him. Was this not what Dante meant in saying that "Art is the *grandchild* of God"?

[5] "The Dyer's Hand," *The Anchor Review*, No. 2 (New York: Doubleday Anchor Books, 1957), pp. 284–85.
[6] *Last Essays* (London: Jonathan Cape, 1941), p. 20.

Theology as Conversation:
With the Sciences and Philosophy

Before one looks for men,
one must have found the Lantern.
—Nietzsche

I   In this chapter I propose to consider two further conversations in which theologians are involved at the present time, those with scientists and philosophers. Obviously we can do no more than touch lightly upon many large and vital themes in a somewhat breathless way. Those who wish to move more carefully and thoroughly across this particular terrain will find suggestions for doing so in the pages that follow. The purpose of this chapter will be realized if the reader is at least made aware of what some of these issues are, and is encouraged to take part in further, more responsible reflection upon them.

The rift or "warfare" (as Andrew D. White called it in his famous book of half a century ago) between science and theology goes even farther back in history than that between theology and the arts. It is already present in the later period of classical Greek thought. But it becomes acute in the early Renaissance as men like Galileo faced within themselves the intense conflict between theological and scientific world-pictures, and it is deepened as Christian thinkers like Pascal feel both threatened and fascinated by "the eternal silence of infinite spaces" opened up by scientific discovery and theory. A long procession of modern thinkers, instanced by such names as Descartes, Locke, Kant, and Hegel, seek to close this gap by putting forward philosophical solutions which harmonize science and religion chiefly by distinguishing them.

Most of us are still familiar with the last phase of this philosophical effort, and there may even be many who remain profoundly influenced by the way in which it set up the problem and moved to solve it. Let me remind you of the approach made by liberal theologians of a generation ago, who were often joined by religiously sensitive scientists in searching for an intellectual concordat or alliance. Put very simply and perhaps a bit crudely, it was something like this. Science deals with facts; religion deals with values. Science describes; religion appreciates. Science is concerned with the *how* of things and events; religion is concerned with the *why* of them. We can have both knowledge and faith so long as they are kept distinct in theory and practice. Then they cannot possibly oppose or seem to cancel out each other.

Therefore one may safely and rightly leave to the scientist the task of measuring and mastering the object-world while looking to the theologian for a delineation of the realm of human values as these are related to the "hypothesis" of God. One must not read the biblical story of creation as if it were geology, or regard Paul's symbol of the body of Christ as if it were biology, or think of Jesus' miracles as if they were medicine. They belong to another and very different realm, that of metaphor rather than measurement and of subjective attachment rather than objective information. Thus the scientist and the theologian can go about their respective business undisturbed, and the "warfare" is brought to a peaceful termination.

Now it must be bluntly said that this attempted solution is no longer pertinent or true, and many of us suspect that it never was. Certainly one must always distinguish in order to relate. Even more important is the warning that theology must allow science free rein in describing objects of whatever kind throughout the length and breadth of the known universe. As Tillich holds, the interfering of theology with the methods and aims of science is destructive for theology itself. So far, so good. Too often in the past Christian theologians have assume the role of King Canute trying to hold back the ocean, protecting areas called miracle or providence from the advancing march of discovery, invention, and technology. This was essentially a strategy of retreat; often it amounted in the words of Einstein to building theological doctrines in the dark spots of scientific research. A perfect example of this method, if it can be called that, was the heralding of Heisenberg's principle of indeterminacy by liberal theologians and some religiously motivated scientists as the vindication of free will in man. They took their cue from science and made the most of it, coming up with a theory which was as full of logical *non sequiturs* as it was offensive to the Christian understanding of human freedom.

What was false and wrong with this older harmonizing answer to the problem of science and religion was that it actually abandoned theological inquiry by assuming the autonomy of science in the determination of what constitutes a fact. Only two alternatives were left open to the theologian. Either he could regard religion as a kind of poetry and mythology and theology as "purely symbolic," or he could try to literalize and accommodate matters of faith to those of scientific fact. Indeed, the two courses often seemed to be the same. The whole perspective of Christian theology was disintegrated by this overly apologetic process, and its entire subject matter was being whittled away to the vanishing point.

This situation has become clearer during the last generation as theology has recovered its balance and reasserted its prerogative as the understanding of the truth of the Christian faith. Not content to build in the dark spots left by science, and unwilling to keep up a rear-guard action against the steady, sometimes staggering march of human knowledge and control of natural forces, theology has been developing its own methods to declare and define its understanding of the world and man in the light of God's centrally and crucially revealing act in Jesus Christ. Without either willfully contradicting science or wistfully accommodating itself to science, theology in recent decades has been rediscovering its own reason for existence and its own right to be heard. Theologians today are not content to restrict themselves to the value-realm so painstakingly marked off by their predecessors.

Their thought ranges widely and freely over every conceivable matter of fact, every zone and facet of the real—nature and history, the known and the unknown, time and eternity, man and God. The only limitation recognized is that of fidelity to the gospel, allegiance to the God who by his Word made the heavens, in whom and through whom and to whom are all things.

There are also reasons coming from outside the Christian faith's own understanding of itself which support this movement in theology toward new wholeness of outlook. Others than theologians have been insisting that the older accommodating dualisms cannot stand, notably Alfred North Whitehead, whose entire lifework was a protest against bifurcating, shelving, or compartmentalizing experienced reality in any way whatsoever. It is no longer possible to maintain a dichotomy between fact and value when fact itself carries the sort of importance and authority which it has for the contemporary world, and when the supposed value-realm of theology has now, thanks chiefly to biblical studies, gotten all tangled up in the web of concrete events and the religious meanings that are inseparable from them. When value is as closely tied to fact as it is in the Christian faith, and when fact per se is given such high value as our present-day deference toward science encourages, then the old, bland, harmonizing effort to divide the two is no longer valid. From both sides we are in a position to see the need for a more unified, and unifying, perspective.

Other neat distinctions have also had to go in recent years. Formerly it was customary to distinguish between pure and applied science. Thus we enabled ourselves to separate scientific research from moral responsibility, rather naïvely believing in the beneficence of expert inquiry as such while forgetting the truth in Bacon's dictum that knowledge is power. Now, however, as everybody knows, the purest science is the most dreadfully applicable of all, and reasonable men begin to wonder if the release of atomic energy may not constitute a kind of trespass against moral and humane principles, perhaps even against the law of God. Neither can we make a comforting distinction between means and ends any longer. Thanks to technological "progress," our means have become precisely our ends, purpose and use are everywhere confused, and "know-how" is widely regarded as the current substitute for wisdom. One might give examples endlessly—the meeting on a significant issue which soon turns into a wrangle over procedure, the much too easy transition from questions of truth or worth to questions of timing and expediency—but the point is so obvious that it does not need to be pressed. It does no good and clarifies nothing to distinguish means from ends unless we realize how frighteningly our means have become ends and our ends have become means in contemporary life. To put the matter in religious terms, a very close connection between technology and idolatry has been made evident in our kind of world.

All this is by way of showing that the older "live and let live" relationship between science and the Christian faith is now very much in doubt. New and agonized questions must be asked about it. The relationship must be thought out afresh by theologians and scientists in an atmosphere of mutual trust and frankness. The urgency of the world situation may provide illumination as well as incentive for such conversations. At all events they should be entered into soon, and seriously, by those who care about the human future and are troubled over the dehumanized world which menaces and manacles us all.

II As a matter of fact such conversations have already begun, carried on by small groups of selected scientists and theologians in Europe and the United States and now reflected in a growing literature on the subject. They have progressed farthest, probably, in matters of common interest to Christian pastors and psychotherapists—namely, those regarding the structuring and functioning of human selfhood as disclosed primarily in feelings of anxiety and guilt. It should not astonish us that attention should be drawn chiefly to these and other pathological manifestations, since they are signally increasing in our time owing to pressures generally felt and recognized. Nor should it be remarkable that a deepened sense of sin in theology finds much in common with the darker view of personality taken by analysts and therapists today.

Thus far theologians have been more ready and willing to learn from the psychotherapists and psychoanalysts than the latter have been to learn from the theologians. An exception is the very recent growth of a viewpoint known as existential psychoanalysis, deriving some of its basic insights from Kierkegaard in particular. Another possible exception is the Jungian psychology, which has always been preoccupied with a "religious factor" in the understanding and treatment of mental illness. By and large, however, the initiative has been taken by thinkers oriented toward the central Christian vision. Tillich is the outstanding example of a thinker who has carefully worked into his theological system principles deliberately drawn from depth psychology and given philosophical and even doctrinal importance. Reinhold Niebuhr, too, finds in the Freudian view of man a telling corroboration of the Christian estimate at many points, while rejecting its "mythology" as a proper substitute for the classical Christian interpretations of Paul, Augustine, or Dante.

Since this particular conversation has already been ably documented in many places we shall not linger upon it here. David Roberts' *Psychotherapy and a Christian View of Man* and Albert Outler's *Psychotherapy and the Christian Message* are indispensable treatments not only in reviewing the conversation but in making significant contributions to it. Other books of well-nigh equal value might be mentioned at some length, especially those by Rollo May and Seward Hiltner. Here we shall confine ourselves to making two very general remarks. The first is that despite numerous efforts the difficulties of translating back and forth between two highly specialized vocabularies are still so great as to be in many cases insurmountable. A single incident may make this plain. Not long ago a teacher of religion and a psychologist were talking to each other on a college campus. The psychologist was asked if he believed in original sin. He quickly replied that he did not, adding, "What is human nature anyway except hair color, skin color, and frustration tolerance?" "Hold on there," said his colleague. "What's that third thing?" The psychologist explained his term by using words like patience, sympathy, trust, and then the teacher of religion knew where he was. He also began to wonder how many problems of communication in this field have their source simply in the fact that we have been clinging to different ways of saying the same thing when common terms in everyday speech might have served us better, at least for the purposes of conversation itself.

For some time to come we shall undoubtedly be in the position of having to learn each other's diverse modes of speech about matters which are, after all, common to us, guarding against indiscriminate borrowing on the one hand and semantic self-enclosure on the other. Especially in the realm of pastoral counseling one must not mistake labeling for analyzing, or confuse preaching to a congregation of one person with diagnosing his inmost needs. A healthy respect for the context of skill and lore out of which words come, whether theological or clinical, is the chief prerequisite here. And at the same time should we not make a more resolute effort to use wherever possible words from our mother tongue which unite rather than divide, with the tang and bite of humanly experienced reality in them? Only so can we break through those protective barrages of specialized jargon which all sorts and conditions of men find it convenient to hide behind when forced to explain themselves to their fellows.

Certain words seem to defy translation or even transposition from one vocabulary into the other. One expects a psychologist to boggle at the word "soul," but just as often he is likely also to rule out the word "self." On the other hand, some words translate much too easily: "God," for example. Of what avail is willingness to use the same word in a conversation when to one of the participants it means infantilism and to the other it means infinity? Some conversations are well along before this comes out through the smooth surface of supposed agreement, and then of course they are quite over and done with.

The second general observation to be made on the progress of the conversation between theology and depth psychology is that if the language barrier can be broken both participants have much to teach each other besides unfamiliar terms. One of the saddest things about contemporary cultural life is the fragmented, isolated character of the professions. One reason is that in a world like ours competence necessarily means specialization, so that after a while it is hard for anyone outside a given profession to know what is being said and thought within it. Theology itself has become professionalized in just this way, to its own great detriment and that of the church at large. Theological work emphatically needs the stringency and accuracy which only a robust encounter with science can give it. A scientifically disciplined mind may help us to lay bare the very logic of theology itself—its characteristic way of working, and the tools of thought and speech with which it works. There is even a sense, and by no means a tenuous or far-fetched one, in which theology may be said to be a science insofar as it is a methodical, reasoned way of making statements about its own subject matter. One may read Barth and Tillich for further details.

If encounter with the sciences, particularly the sciences of man, can help to clarify the theologian's use of rational methods, it is also true that theology can bring a needed corrective to scientific ways of working. Since it deals frankly and deliberately with mysteries beyond man's exact knowledge and expert control, it must resist any kind of logical strait-jacketing or foreshortening of its perspective, by psychology in particular. A theological critique of psychology would need first of all to expose the working assumptions—themselves unproved but surely implied—by which the psychologist carries on his enterprise. What constitutes, for him, a "fact"? To what extent does he merely describe facts and in what degree does he attempt to explain them? Does such explanation, in his view, consist in a process of reducing or factoring out rather than giving reasons that are commensurable with the phenomena they purport to explain? Again, is not such a reduction of the human to the natural in some sense a denial of the human, a substituting of the manageable for the mysterious? This is the line which might be taken by a theologian in conversation with a psychologist; some bias may be apparent on both sides, but the primary aim is that of bringing assumptions out in the open, to which neither party should object.

We have of course been speaking of the necessary preliminaries to this conversation rather than the heart of it. That would include discussion of matters and issues such as human freedom and responsibility taken from the benevolently neutral but common ground of ethics. It would not be a question of whether one denied freedom or affirmed it, but of what one could conceivably mean by it or what equivalents he would propose for getting on with the age-old debate. It should be possible to make some headway in this area once the ground rules of discussion have become clarified and accepted. Emmanuel Mounier, in *The Character of Man*, has made an impressive effort to do just this; and the books by Roberts and Outler mentioned earlier belong in the same category.

Conversations are also taking place between Christian theologians and the social scientists. Two questions have emerged as having signal importance, one regarding the meaning of history and the other concerned with the conception of community. Theologians have always been interested in the question about history. But when Christian historians like Herbert Butterfield or Marjorie Reeves ask whether we can speak of history as a whole with something like plan or purpose in it, a new dimension is added to the discussion which is lacking in the work of men like Reinhold Niebuhr and Karl Löwith, who come at it from outside the historical discipline itself. Butterfield's idea of Providence especially commends itself as a genuine wrestling with the problem of two perspectives on a common theme.[1] The question is now raised whether we can even think of history as contrasted with a congeries of "trends" or "movements" apart from presuppositions which are at bottom theological, involving belief, however disguised or dim, in an oversight and agency very like what Christians mean by God.

On the matter of human community there have been unexpected convergences as sociology has become more philosophical and theology has gotten more churchly in orientation. Buber's distinction between "I-Thou" and "I-it" relations has been influential, as have the positions of George Herbert Mead, Charles Hartshorne, H. Richard Niebuhr, Talcott Parsons, and others who have not been content merely to describe human relationships but are determined to understand them. Here once more the basic question appears to be whether human community can be properly regarded as the resultant of needs and drives within the human animal compounded with illusions and distortions peculiar to man, or whether community—even as an idea—includes elements which can be accounted for only on the supposition of man's free, self-transcending search for fulfillment and harmony with his fellow men. In short, is it animal pressure or spiritual possibility that defines community? The question, plainly, is not a simple either-or, since no analysis of human relations can be undertaken which rules out in advance one or the other of these types of explanation; but the matter of emphasis is after all extremely important. To a theologian it is very significant that the old

[1] See his *Christianity and History* (New York: Scribner's, 1950), chap. V.

hard line between descriptive sociology and social ethics is becoming thinner and softer; terms like "egoism" and "altruism" are being rephrased and rethought sociologically and anthropologically; and everywhere within the social sciences the ancient question "What is man?" is being earnestly and expertly asked. This makes possible the sort of conversation which has not been entered into since the time of Auguste Comte, as questions which one thought forever closed are now reopened by thinkers on both sides of what has long seemed an impassable gulf.

III   It is, however, with the natural scientists that theological conversation is at once most urgent and most fundamental—not only because the natural sciences provide the models and methods which are used in all the sciences, but also because in them the very character of scientific intelligence and endeavor is singularly disclosed. Natural science is in fact the meaning and intent of all science, taken in its broadest sense as "generalized, verified, systematized knowledge." And since it is just here that the sharpest questions have been raised for thoughtful people the world over, during the last fifteen years especially, it is also here that conversation should take place.

Many treatments of matters lying within the scope of this conversation between Christian theology and natural science have already appeared, and more are to come. They range all the way from tracts for the times, occasioned by the nightmarish use of atomic power for military purposes, to massive studies of the theoretical relationships and implications of the disciplines involved. Both kinds of work need to be done, but probably the most generally useful books are those in the middle range which consider some particular doctrine in the light of scientific thinking and achievement or else address themselves to some aspect of scientific method or viewpoint seen in the context of wider human concerns or experiences.

We shall have opportunity only to make comments on one topic of this latter kind with the hope that those who are interested in going farther may find in this chapter the incentive for doing so. To engage in this conversation of theology with natural science is by no means an easy task. One must take the risk of having his own intellectual foundations really shaken and his cherished convictions destroyed. This is as true when one happens to be a scientist who believes firmly in the beneficence of all experimental investigation as when one is by vocation a Christian thinker who is accustomed to see in every human situation or condition a kind of argument for God.

Our topic, perhaps the most weighty for the future of the conversation we are reviewing, has to do with the meaning of the word "nature" itself. Scientists do not talk much about nature as such, but they assume it constantly. Their attention is directed to processes and patterns of behavior on a multitude of levels from the subatomic to the galactic. Yet underneath the variegated and multitudinous researches which make up the intricate web of natural science there persists the ancient, universal conception of the uniformity of nature. Hydrogen always behaves like hydrogen, wherever it is isolated, controlled, and examined. True, the so-called laws of nature do not *make* anything happen as it does; but even as generalizations based on a high statistical probability they presuppose, if not some kind of cosmic compulsion, at least a world which in significant respects is a whole whose aspects can be read off with a fair degree of knowability. Experiments can be repeated and their conclusions checked in different places or periods of time; and this repeatability implies regularity "out there" in what is being looked at and described. Measurements really measure; equations actually equate; symbols genuinely symbolize. To the scientist, then, nature means not an all-embracing totality with laws determining the behavior of every part, but nonetheless an observable, knowable uniformity which logically makes science itself possible. Perhaps the best single, shorthand definition of nature is "the way things are," to borrow the title of a recent major volume by the Harvard physicist Percy W. Bridgman.

But where the scientist says "nature" the theologian says "creation." Things are the way they are, according to this essential Christian doctrine, for a very good reason; they do not merely happen without cause. That reason, or cause, is to be found not so much in natural events and objects themselves—although they contain hints and traces of it—but in an ordering agency which is beyond and above them and therefore in some degree disclosed in them. This, as Thomas Aquinas would say, is what everyone means by God. Incidentally, one does not have to agree with his particular formulation of the cosmological argument to grant the theologian his point that nature is not self-explanatory, that things do not give a reason by and for themselves. Their reason is to be found, Christians believe in common with the whole monotheistic tradition of Western culture, in the design or purpose of an ultimate, transcendent reality which explains them without being explained by them.

The Christian view of nature as creation must always be stated symbolically, since we too are creatures whose existence is woven firmly into the web of natural fact. Bounded in time and space, we can only use the tokens that we know for suggesting the relation of the world to God. So we say "Father," but we do not mean that God begets the world; or we say "Maker," but we do not mean that God makes the world the way a carpenter makes a box. In a recent helpful volume Langdon Gilkey has carefully expounded the phrase in the Apostles' Creed "Maker of heaven and earth" so as to remove all possible misunderstandings coming from prescientific literalism, while insisting upon the validity of Christian image and metaphor in setting forth what nature conceived as creation does mean. We must mean more than we can possibly manage to say about God, and this too we must somehow attempt to say.

This referring of the world of nature back to God, which is the major intent of the doctrine of creation, is not a threadbare theory of how the universe began, but a statement in frankly mythical and poetic terms of what Christians believe to be the most significant truth about nature—that it *is* a whole because it is willed, called into being, by the one true God. Creation did not happen once upon a time, since it includes time; it is not our word for a past act of God but for a constant feature of God's dealing with us and his world. God is forever the Creator, and the world is in every moment and part to be known as his creation. In the biblical and Christian world-picture, this conviction that the world is a realm of creaturely dependence upon God is put in terms of a primordial derivation from God's will because this is the most powerful and appropriate symbol for dependence. It is the one sure way of guarding against the views of pantheism and deism, views, incidentally, which have often appealed to men of science when they faced these ultimate questions—the first sees God related to nature as internal to it, the second sees God as externally related to it. Neither theory—and these are theories, in contrast to the doctrines of our Christian faith—can do justice to our deep and lasting intuition that the God in whom we believe is both immanent in and transcendent to the world of nature.

Our thought about God is necessarily and consciously anthropomorphic, just as our thought concerning man must be theomorphic, since it does take God to account for the kind of being-in-the-world which is man. We answer the charges of the Freudians and Marxists simply by granting their force and then by showing why the Christian myth is more adequate to the known facts and the believed truths than any possible theory of origin. In these days, one may employ the language of myth and poetry only because he knows what he is doing, and why. In large part theology is the justifying of the Christian vision of the world to the rational intelligence—that is, the giving of reasons for the faith that is in us. It is not necessarily, as so many otherwise sophisticated persons seem to think, rationalization in the bad and Freudian sense, which has very little of reason in it.

The Christian understanding of nature as creation is neither antiscientific nor prescientific, though in some respects it may well be postscientific. It accepts, because it logically requires, the working assumptions of the natural sciences regarding the regularity and uniformity of their data as well as the reliability of their findings. There is thus no quarrel with science as to what the facts are; the whole issue raised by theology concerns what the facts mean. In this respect, it is true, theology ranges itself with the humanities in the great debate which is shaping up at the present time vis-à-vis the sciences. Theology's purposeful use of image and symbol, its deliberate attention to mysteries rather than problems, and its reliance upon tokens of participation rather than techniques of observation all put theology—at least provisionally and procedurally—on the side of the humanities. In order to complete the picture one would also need to show how theology differs from the humanities, but this would carry us far afield from the present topic.

Before we leave the doctrine of creation there is, however, a further aspect of it which deserves mention in relation to the natural sciences. When the Christian theologian speaks of nature as God's creation, he means not only that nature is an argument for God but also that it is a sacrament of God. This way of putting the matter, borrowed from John Baillie, suggests strongly that nature is somehow capable of showing forth its divine origin and goal, that it is viable to God's presence as well as to his power. The Old Testament expresses this conviction in the most vivid way imaginable by picturing trees clapping their hands, hills skipping like lambs, stars singing together—all creation shouting for joy in praise of its Creator. In Christian terms, nature is not an inert medium for God to break through in his search for man; it is instead, as in so much of van Gogh's painting, the very avenue of God's grace and the very accompaniment of man's praise. In this conception, therefore, man and nature are related not as subject to object or as part to whole; man is at once more natural, as nature is more humane, than science-dominated philosophies allow; and creatureliness or existence under God binds both together, giving both such being and meaning as they have.

As Whitehead wrote, a dead nature gives no reasons. In the Christian view, on the other hand, nature is eminently alive; it is not, in Gabriel Marcel's words, a desert of objects to be itemized and analyzed. But what gives life to nature is that it is grounded in the living God and capable of making response, on many levels and in ways appropriate to these levels, to its ground of being. Karl Heim's notion of dimensions may seem fanciful to some, but it can be useful in articulating within the context of modern science the historic Christian affirmation of the orders of being, to which Augustine, Thomas Aquinas, and Pascal made such memorable contributions. Thus it may be said that both the accuracy of science and the ardor of faith are needed in order to understand the world ordained for man to live in—a world whose very nature consists in its creaturely, serviceable relationship to God.

Can the scientist and the theologian agree in principle on this conception of nature as open upward to God? Probably not, at least at first. Many scientists would doubtless argue that they do not even need the idea of a unitary or at any rate uniform nature; but as we have seen, their very method speaks out tellingly against their skeptical caution at this point. The basic issue here, I think, is not whether nature can be *thought* as a single idea but whether it is not the tacit presupposition of all investigation and formulation in the sciences. If it is such a presupposition, then the question at once becomes this: Is nature to be regarded as a "nothing but" category, an all-embracing and all-sufficient synonym for everything there is, or is it rather the case that we can only include nature, in the sense of "the way things are," by a principle of understanding that transcends it as well? One may not have to be some sort of traditional supernaturalist to answer with the latter alternative; but neither does one cease completely to be scientific if he gives this answer. That is really the chief point a Christian theologian, engaged in conversation with the natural scientist, would wish to make.

IV We turn now to a review of the conversations going on between theology and the two types of philosophy most dominant today, analytical philosophy and existential philosophy.

For many years theology and the movement known as logical analysis had very little if any contact with each other. True, there were occasional brushes of an acrimonious and disdainful kind, but no sustained discussion of the areas of disagreement. So-called "logical positivists" were fond of asserting that all theological propositions were "meaningless," having neither real semantic reference nor operational fruitfulness. The work of the logical positivists did constitute in their own eyes a standing critique and refutation of all metaphysics, of which they believed theology to be a part. Men like A. J. Ayer proposed that metaphysics be eliminated from philosophy by setting up a standard of meaning which would rule out in advance all metaphysical statements. This was the famous (or infamous!) verification principle: in order to have meaning, any statement must be either analytic (that is, true by definition) or empirical (that is, verifiable to sense experience). Propositions in logic or mathematics, plus of course all definitions, fall within the first class. They say nothing about the real world but only about the way in which given symbols are to be used. To the second class belong both scientific hypotheses and many common-sense statements, which convey genuine information and can be tested by the verification principle. Since most

of the statements made in metaphysics, ethics, or theology fall
within neither class, they were therefore called by Ayer "nonsensical pseudo-propositions"; they lacked any meaning whatsoever in
his predetermined sense.

But this view of the matter could not possibly last long. To class
as nonsense all sorts of things that people were always saying
had the effect, quite naturally, of raising far more questions than
it answered. The positivist, to be sure, could explain that he was
using the word "nonsense" in a highly technical and not necessarily disparaging way; he sometimes granted that theologians were
capable of talking very profound nonsense indeed! But soon it
became clear that, instead of applying one all-out standard for
distinguishing the meaningful from the meaningless, one could
actually be both more analytical and more empirical in recognizing
different sorts of meaning in different kinds of statements.

Those philosophers who now adopt this latter approach are no
longer positivists. They have replaced the *assertion* "The meaning
of a statement is the method of its verification" by the *question*
"What is the logic of it? How does it actually go?" Implied here
is the belief that every statement has, or can be shown to have,
its own logic. These analytical philosophers have consciously
parted company with the earlier positivists. They do not advance
a world-view or a methodology which is in obvious, deliberate
conflict with the Christian faith. They do not rule out in advance
theological statements as nonsensical or meaningless, chiefly because they have too many interesting questions to ask about them.
What is more, they ask these questions just as they would inquire
about the logic of any kind of statement. In short, they are not
engaged in attacking but in analyzing.

As Basil Mitchell writes, "It would be a very unempirical em-
piricist who presumed to pronounce, in advance of careful investigation, that the claims of theology were unfounded, and a very
complacent theologian who expected to learn nothing from a
philosophical movement which has brought needed clarification
into other disciplines."[2] This remark indicates where matters stand
at the present time, and is borne out by study of the published
work of groups engaged in continuous discussion of theological
language from the analytical point of view. Above all, they raise

[2] Basil Mitchell, *Faith and Logic* (London: Allen & Unwin, 1957), pp. 5-6.

the question "How does this sort of talk go, and what is it trying to do?" Although logical analysts are often keenly critical of what seem to them to be obscurities and gratuitous mystification in theology, they are by no means bent on the reduction or elimination of theological meaning. On the contrary, they wish to discover it. Their aim is to clarify, not to expose or to explain away.

Moreover, these philosophers do not hesitate to discuss topics close to the heart of the theological enterprise itself, such as "the soul," "the grace of God," "creation," "miracles," and "death." Here not only is language examined but issues are joined, not only are meanings assigned but truths are assessed. These thinkers are involved in the ancient theological task of faith-seeking-understanding, although they might prefer to call it understanding-seeking-faith.

The present stage of this conversation can hardly be called a consensus, but at least it represents a quite remarkable convergence of two formerly divergent, not to say mutually uncomprehending, viewpoints. This convergence has several important truths to teach theologians themselves. One is that the clarification of Christian language, whether scriptural, liturgical, or doctrinal, is itself a theological duty. It was none other than Karl Barth who wrote, back in 1936, that the task of theology is "to criticize and revise language about God by the principle of the standard peculiar to the Church."[3] True, there may be a considerable difference between a theologian's interest in such criticism and revision and that of an analytical philosopher, who would find it hard to grant the relevance of "the standard peculiar to the Church." But our point here is simply that both are fundamentally concerned with the matter of language, that is, the question of how and why certain things are said and what is actually meant by them. There is thus no impassable gulf or basic opposition arising out of the subject matter itself. Theology and analytical philosophy converge on the same target, although they are launched from very different points of view. Therefore it is worth while to insist that theology, no less than philosophical analysis, deals with the propriety and adequacy of its own language and so cannot receive too much help from those whose announced purpose is so like its own.

[3] *The Doctrine of the Word of God* (Edinburgh, 1936), p. 6.

Indeed, recent neo-orthodox thinkers have been strenuously trying to recover and adopt traditional biblical and creedal language, to such an extent that theology sometimes appears to be no more than Christian ideology or propaganda. This is an impression, however, which it is always a theologian's purpose to erase. Lest the Christian faith become a matter of using warmed-over stereotypes, we must ceaselessly re-examine the color, weight, and texture of the words and images we employ. While there must be a "special language" for elucidating and communicating our faith, it should not become so special that it claims to be beyond criticism and above inspection from whatever quarter other than the Christian community itself. Theological language needs spaciousness as well as specificity; it should be humanly relevant no less than Christianly recognizable.

A second thing to be learned from this convergence of logical analysis and theology is that one cannot for long address himself to the problem of Christian language without coming up against the matter of Christian truth. The philosophical analyst may start out as a kind of speech therapist who is attempting to correct the verbal contortions of religious people, but soon he is inevitably drawn into a genuine concern with what is being said and why, as well as "how it goes." This is the natural result of a continuous and deepening conversation in which an analyst's much-prized objectivity is more and more replaced by empathy; it is in fact the tendency in any study of the logic of any kind of statement.

Hence, although the analytical philosopher may begin with a disinclination to believe in the truth of what theologians are saying, he may soon discover that his concentration on the "how" of theological talk opens out upon a sympathetic understanding of the "why" of it. There may be some good reasons for this tendency. One is that a word is never a mere word; in giving his word a human being gives himself. His language, moreover, is not simply personal but structural; it is symptomatic and expressive of his own situation with respect to others, the world, and himself. As the Quakers say, a word is always suggestive of the place where words come from, and as such it carries with it a unity of word, thought, and person. One may even say with considerable justice that the word *is* the person and his thought. As William Zuurdeeg writes, language means not only words and sentences but "man-who-speaks."[4]

Another reason why questions of meaning always tend to become questions of being is more theological in character. For the Christian faith, man's power of using and of being moved by language has its roots in his relationship as creature to the creating God. It signifies, in Brunner's phrase, that man is addressable by God. A Christian theologian can scarcely converse with an analytical philosopher without making some such tacit assumption; and if the philosopher may not at once be able to affirm the same presupposition, he should not deny it out of hand either, unless he wishes to step quite outside his analytical role.

We may in fact consider the major doctrines of the Christian faith in this light as exemplifying a certain "philosophy of language." Does not the action of God in creating, revealing, and redeeming have from first to last to do with speaking and hearing, commanding and obeying, initiating and responding? "And God said . . . ," "Thus saith the Lord . . . ," "In the beginning was the Word . . . ," "It has been said . . . but I say unto you"— these are among the most characteristic of biblical statements which a Christian theologian has to interpret and render intelligible. The "logic" of such statements would surely seem to be that the relationship between God and man is both a communicating and a communicable one. Hence Christian theology, as Barth never tires of saying, is necessarily a theology of the Word. In this light, and under the prodding of logical analysis, new impetus is given to the old debates concerning symbol and image, metaphor and myth, analogy and paradox, name and reality. Parenthetically, it is amazing how contemporaneous and pertinent some medieval disputations and treatises on these topics now turn out to be.

In the third place, what does this current conversation have to teach us on the theological side regarding the old question of how theology is related to philosophy? Clearly, it poses this question in a new and forceful manner. If a theologian thinks that analytical philosophy gives him *carte blanche* to go on using the language of faith without having to face disturbing epistemological,

4 William Zuurdeeg, *An Analytical Philosophy of Religion* (Nashville: Abingdon, 1958), p. 19.

ethical, or metaphysical issues, he is sadly mistaken. Theology, by its own account, is not only faith-talk but truth-talk. Therefore a theologian who comes into fruitful contact with linguistic analysis should become more philosophical, not less so. He must take up seriously the task of clarifying the meaning of Christian words, thus justifying their use to those both within and outside the Christian churches. He should also try to define the ground rules of theological and religious communication, showing why it is necessary to speak in symbol and myth and setting forth so far as possible the rationale of such communication. Finally, the theologian must be willing to compare his own kind of speech with other modes of theological expression in terms of the varying philosophical axioms and angles of vision which clearly condition them all. In short, theologians need to become more analytical themselves; they must avoid the pitfalls of a theological positivism which mistakes bare assertion for profound conviction.

This would surely represent a valid and telling response on the part of theologians to the new temper and tendency in philosophy. The Christian churches, on whose behalf the theologian speaks, cannot safely escape coming to grips with any influential philosophy, unless they are willing to be deemed irrelevant and given to what the analysts call "double-think." Not only the good name of the churches but the truth-claim which inheres in the Christian gospel itself forbids the taking of such an easy and ignoble path by theologians.

V   The other pole in current philosophy is represented by existentialism, which on one side is a vigorous protest against the analytical rationalism and scientism of our century. As a matter of fact, this protest is not an "ism" at all, and we shall better speak of it as existential philosophy. What we must try to desig-nate is a movement rather than a position in contemporary thought; that is, we do not find a group of thinkers bound to-gether by a common set of beliefs, an accepted method of inquiry, and a shared program of intellectual reconstruction. The people to whom the word "existential" is applied do not make up a mutual admiration society but often find that their sharpest dis-agreements are among themselves, not between themselves and all others. Neither do they go back to some one man's original work as disciples develop, correct, and expand the thought of a revered teacher—although Kierkegaard comes close to serving this function for some existentialists. They do not form as closely knit a group as the Boston personalists, for example, nor do they issue manifestoes like the religious humanists in former years, though Jean-Paul Sartre is correct in finding affinities between these viewpoints. In other words, what we are dealing with here is a kind of stress or approach within today's polyphony of thought.

So much for negatives. But what is this stress, and how may its presence be detected? Our difficulty in pinning it down follows largely from the character of the accent itself. More than any other sort of thinker, the existentialist keeps a strong sense of the element of personal response within his statements and the style in which he makes them. He knows himself to be, in Augustine's words, a question to himself—a question which can scarcely be answered until it is really asked and heard. The sort of thinker about whom we are talking thinks *himself*, as if his life depended upon it, which it does, and as if to live and to think were after all the same thing, which they are. The tone and accent of the existentialist, then, is found not so much in the answers he gives as in the questions he asks. What does it mean to exist? Who am I, really? What am I to being?

This is the kind of questioning all existential thinkers have in common, if that may be called common which divides and individualizes men. The existential point of view is at bottom a questioning of man by himself, a monologue which soon turns into a dialogue between man and what Tillich terms "being itself." The existential accent can be discovered and traced by certain marks— a keen awareness of human contingency or the "might-have-been-otherness" of everything we do and are; an equally sharp recognition of the limitations of reason as an instrument for answering the final questions (since the question which I put to being is ultimately that which being puts to me); a poignant feeling for the fact that one is bounded and determined by the situations into which he is thrown, situations which always have the double character of promise and menace, opportunity and obstacle; and a resolution to maintain in thought the same degree of urgency, tentativeness, and radical humility which is required in human life itself.

Existentialism, as William James remarked about pragmatism, is actually a new name for a very old way of thinking. Socrates with his "know thyself" is certainly one of its progenitors, and the Stoics, and Augustine—especially the Augustine of the *Confessions* and the *Soliloquies*, who said he wanted to know only two things, God and the soul. Perhaps Western philosophy has never been without an existentialist strain, dormant or active; but in the modern period, above all in Pascal and Kierkegaard, this way of thinking becomes what James again would call a "live option" defined against alternative viewpoints.

We are chiefly interested, however, in contemporary forms, and from a theological perspective there are two—the Christian and the atheistic. The Christian is of course the older and stronger, so that even atheists and skeptics who ally themselves with the existentialist way of thinking tend to make parodies out of the testimonies of our faith. In reading the non-Christian existentialists one has the sense that his own convictions are being set forth, but in a strangely inverted or distorted way, so that they become almost but never quite unrecognizable. Here one finds freedom without responsibility, guilt without judgment, the fall without the creation, hell without heaven. This is why the Christian thinker should not merely fight such existentialism or attempt to contradict it; but at the same time he should not simply accept its reading of the human situation as it stands, as if it could be made the Christian's own. There may be a clue for understanding this strange character of atheistic existentialism *vis-à-vis* Christian faith in Albert Camus's point that to revolt against something is to say both Yes and No to it; this kind of existential thinking is just such a revolt.

What is important for the theologian to remember, then, is that existential philosophy, precisely because it is not a position so much as an approach, is ambiguous from a Christian viewpoint. As Father Roger Troisfontaines has written, it may become either a religious philosophy in support of the Christian faith or on the other hand the most anti-Christian philosophy that could be conceived. One can understand why Gabriel Marcel, for example, does not like to be called an existentialist, which confuses him in the popular mind with Sartre and tends to vitiate everything Marcel is attempting to achieve. Or take the case of Karl Jaspers, which is singularly instructive. One would have to call him an existentialist if any designation were to be used; but Jaspers remains in many respects an old-style agnostic, uncommitted one way or the other so far as the religious option is concerned.

Yet the ambiguity may prove to be fortunate, at least for theological purposes of conversation at the present time, for reasons which I shall try to indicate. The stance of a Christian theologian toward any going philosophical viewpoint can never be that of sheer avoidance or distaste; one's thought is always deviously influenced by what one thinks he has to fight or deny. At the same time, one can never simply take over the framework of such a philosophy for theological purposes without in some measure abandoning his own faith-perspective, as was shown in liberalism's use of philosophical idealism at the turn of the present century and earlier, or in the dependence of medieval scholasticism upon Aristotle. The ambiguity within existentialism may be fortunate if it prevents the Christian thinker from either swallowing it whole or rejecting it out of hand, as many are tempted to do.

As we have already remarked in connection with analytical philosophy, Christian theologians will find it difficult to say a simple Yes or No to existentialism. We have much to learn from it, and there are even some issues confronting thoughtful men and women today on which we may take a common stand with it. In the first place, existentialism, like romanticism before it, is a valid and robust protest against the widespread idolizing of science in the modern world. Whether he is a man of religious faith or not, the existentialist is very likely to put forth the claims of human freedom and uniqueness, as against the rationalizing and pragmatizing tendencies which are encouraged by the uncritical—and unscientific—attitude of multitudes of people toward the truly impressive achievements of science. Must not a theologian stand shoulder to shoulder with existentialists of whatever persuasion in defending what Kierkegaard called "the existing individual" against what appears to be a dominating trend of contemporary thought and life?

Christianity, like existentialism, is mightily concerned with what it is and means to be a man. From whatever quarter it may come, theologians should welcome insight into the human character and condition; and existentialist thought is peculiarly rich in such insights. The generally prevailing American notion that the Christian faith is synonymous with optimism about man's dignity and essential goodness needs the drastic corrective of a way of viewing man which keeps its eye upon the dark forces of anxiety, guilt, and death. No good can possibly come of trying to avoid facing what is vulnerable, irrational, or demonic in human existence. "Man is a great deep, and the hairs of his head are more easily to be numbered than the motions of his heart," as Augustine wrote long ago. This depth in man, which Christians have traditionally called spirit, is the root of both his grandeur and his misery. Existential philosophy commends itself to theologians on the ground that while it emphasizes the distinctively human as against the pervasively natural (as in Sartre's contrast between what is "in-itself" and what is "for-itself"), it does not magnify or glorify this difference in an unrealistic and un-Christian fashion.

This movement in contemporary thought also deserves theological notice and assessment for its contribution to the understanding of the faith-reason relationship. Existentialists are widely supposed to be irrationalists or anti-rationalists, and it is true that in their writings may be found many strictures and negative verdicts upon the pretensions of rationalism. But we must not forget that other philosophical viewpoints over the last fifty years have been making similar judgments, and also that it is not the exercise of reason itself but the inordinate reliance upon abstract structures and speculative systems that is here suspect. Some intemperate and exaggerated things have certainly been said by existentialists concerning reason, but their fundamental point is clearly well taken. Subjectivity may not be truth, as in the famous dictum of Kierkegaard; however, it may yield dimensions and aspects of truth which objectivity can never fathom, and without which our knowledge may be less than wisdom.

Here the great merit of existentialism has been its insistence that philosophy does not have to limit itself to the forms of technical or systematic reason. It may adopt other means of communication such as vision, metaphor, meditations, aphorisms, or notebooks. Existentialists are thoroughly committed to the view that in searching for truth in ultimate matters the whole human being, not merely his mind or reason, is passionately involved. He must therefore be aroused and personally engaged, for truth yields itself only to engagement, not detachment, to reflection and intro-spection and not to classification and definition. It is not by ob-servation but by participation that the world surrenders its secret and bestows its blessing. Hence in the degree to which existential-ism makes effective the use of the language of personal involve-ment, as in drama or poetry, it approaches the language of reli-gious faith and tends to overcome the gap between Christian com-mitment and philosophical understanding which has proved so disastrous in the modern world. It is even possible, and men like Marcel are already showing us the way, that out of the contact of theology with existentialism may emerge a new and significant kind of Christian philosophy, which will have a flexibility and a maneuverability greatly needed in the years ahead.

A final benefit to be conferred by existential philosophy upon Christian theology is the way in which it brings home to us the genuine risk bound up in faith itself. One cannot confront exis-tentialism honestly if he thinks it simply poses the human questions to which he has the "Christian answer." One must not only hear the question to which he hopes to give the answer; he must enter into the question, making it in some real sense his own. This means that he will not remain safely behind the barriers of his own convictions and assurances but will venture forth, as David Roberts says in the best book on this subject, "to the point of self-identification with those to whom, after all, God is not a premise but a question or a target."[5] The risk of exposure to unfaith is always that of having one's cherished formulations of the truth shattered, of experiencing radical doubt within oneself. What the theologian must never forget is that faith itself is that kind of risk, or "wager," as Pascal called it, which cannot be too sharply dis-tinguished from a tidy, cozy battery of answers to the human predicament.

In our first two chapters we have been attempting to do just this. By now it is perhaps plain that the nature and task of the-ology as conversation stems directly from the character of the Christian faith itself. That faith is always and inevitably a risky business. It involves us in unforeseen outcomes and unpremedi-tated conclusions. Without destroying our zeal for sharing and witnessing to the truth as we have found it in Christ, it gives us

[5] In *Existentialism and Religious Belief* (New York: Oxford, 1957), p. 338.

the capacity and readiness for exposure and entrance to the world-mind. If therefore one wished to build a program for theology as conversation, he could do no better than to heed the great words of the apostle Paul, "I am made all things to all men, that by all means I might save some." This has not been a favorite text in the theology of the last twenty or twenty-five years. Other maxims of Paul have been extracted and lifted up by theologians, but this one has been curiously neglected. Yet in our own time, when we must move forward to re-explore and repossess the lost provinces of human culture for the Lordship of Christ, this principle of self-identification becomes highly pertinent and indeed imperative. "To the weak I became as weak," wrote Paul again. In a sermon commenting on this passage there are some unforgettable words of Tillich: "The real theologian is he who has the strength to perceive and to confess his weakness, so that his is the victory."[6] In this very confessing of our weakness as theologians, in this willing encounter with what may seem at first to be inimical to faith, is to be found our victory, which if it may be God will win through us in our own day and generation.

[6] Paul Tillich, *The Shaking of the Foundations* (New York: Scribner's, 1948), p. 125.

Theology as Interpretation

*O the depths of the riches both of the wisdom and
the knowledge of God!*
—Romans 11:33

In addition to carrying on the kind of conversations which we have been overhearing, theologians are also minding their own business. Since the business of theology has always been largely that of interpretation, it will repay us to look rather closely at the ways in which traditional elements within the Christian faith are being restated today. Especially significant in this whole enterprise is the matter of biblical interpretation. This constitutes the ground or base to which theologians must always return, however far away their conversations with other disciplines and interests may sometimes take them. In this sense all theology is biblical theology.

But this ancient theological task is undertaken at the present time with some decidedly new approaches and results. What "biblical theology" has come to mean today is both more and less than scriptural interpretation in the older sense. It means more, in that it insists not only upon understanding the Bible theologically, but upon understanding theology biblically; and it means less, in that it tends to stay much closer to restatement and retelling, than the word "interpretation" normally connotes. The time has come, I believe, for taking a long, hard look at this entire movement in contemporary theology, asking where it is leading us and what the next steps are likely to be. Granted that theology must be interpretation of the Christian Scriptures, what ought we to mean by interpretation? That is the question with which we shall be dealing in this chapter.

One of the main points to be made is that theological interpretation differs very greatly from mere translation or "recital" of the deeds of God set forth in the Bible. I should like to build my case for this view rather slowly and carefully. In the first place, we shall need to remind ourselves of the recent convergence between biblical and theological studies. Then we shall try to specify some of the main emphases in what goes by the name of biblical theology today. Thirdly, a question must be asked about this movement which I believe to be significant and penetrating. In the fourth place, we shall be concerned with the relationship between revelation and communication. And finally we have to inquire whether out of all this experience and the facing of these issues we can construct once more anything like a Christian doctrine of the Word.

I As is generally recognized, our present theological renaissance goes back at least thirty years, to the publication of Karl Barth's commentary on Paul's letter to the Romans. That highly influential book ushered in the tendency which usually is known on this side of the Atlantic as "neo-orthodoxy"—a designation which perhaps reveals as much about the namers of the movement as about the thing named. It was fifteen years and more before neo-orthodoxy began to win disciples in the Anglo-Saxon countries. Many of us who studied in seminaries here during the thirties were taught the Old and New Testaments in a way which introduced us to all kinds of fascinating archaeological data, highly critical reservations, and intriguing hypothetical reconstructions of original documents. But with what we then understood to be theology, all this had very little to do. And our classes in theology were likely to be as unbiblical as those in Bible were untheological. Hence we were quite ill prepared to teach or preach in line with the convergence that was developing on the Continent. We had considerable work of our own to do before we could assimilate or understand just what was going on abroad.

Of course, things are very different now. We take for granted the importance, relevance, and authority of Scripture for all theological endeavor. And this means far more than that every theological conclusion should find support and illustration within the biblical writings, more even than that theology should be surrounded with biblical images and idioms. What biblical theology has been teaching us is that theology as such is to be informed and structured by the motifs, categories, perspectives of Scripture itself. It should not simply refer back or rest ultimately upon the Bible, but must be impregnated, saturated, and even controlled by the very life, world, and faith of the Bible. Otherwise, we are told, it is not Christian theology at all.

There is a further point made by the biblical theologians, although not so clearly or explicitly as the first. It is the necessity of a frankly theological viewpoint and approach for any Christian interpretation of the Bible, and especially for historical and critical work within the biblical field. This point has not been made as well or as strongly as the first, possibly because it did not seem as important or essential at the time. Now, however, it needs to be accented firmly and indelibly, for reasons which will soon be made plain.

But at the moment let us dwell upon the major emphases within this insistence that all theological work should be shaped and structured by the biblical understanding of religious faith. First of all, there is certainly an awakened sense of man-in-community as defining and unifying the Old and New Testaments. This community is grounded in a covenant which God makes with man—a relationship which has sometimes been called triadic or triangular by geometrical-minded theologians—a relationship in which man's responsibility toward his fellows is defined as proceeding from his responsibility to God. Entire systems of Christian ethics have been constructed on this horizontal-vertical scheme. Human rights and duties have been deduced from the divine claim and command, following consciously or unconsciously the books of the law in the Old Testament.

This covenant-founded, covenant-formed community is seen by many biblical theologians as the unifying theme of both Testaments. It is said to establish a degree of continuity between them hitherto unsuspected—between the synagogue and the church, between the old and the new Israel, between Adam and Christ, between law and gospel. Thus the Bible is regarded as a single book, recounting a single history and proclaiming a single message. What liberal theology separated, biblical theology thinks back together again. Historical continuity spells literary, and theological, unity.

There can be no doubt that this insistence upon the fundamental unity of Scripture is salutary and true in many ways. But it should not lead to the blurring of necessary distinctions between Judaism and Christianity. After all, there is a basic and essential difference which neither the Christianizing of the Old Testament nor the Judaizing of the New can possibly remove. One learns very soon not to make quick verbal or ideological distinctions between the Old and the New Testament. But one can hardly be a Christian theologian without having to insist that there is a genuine, profound distinction to be made. From the viewpoint of our Christian faith, the difference is that between prophecy and fulfillment, preparation and consummation, anticipation and realization. And plainly, it is Jesus Christ who makes this difference. Continuity there surely is, at many points astonishing, but unity in the theological sense is something else again.

This whole issue is further complicated by the fact that we do not use the words "Old Testament" and "New Testament" in a single, unambiguous sense. They do not refer merely to the grouping of biblical books within the literary canon established by the Christian church during the early centuries of its history. They also have a significance which is essentially theological, and this is by no means identical with literary or chronological divisions. Thus within the books of the Old Testament there is, quite clearly, a new covenant of promise which justifies their being included in the Christian Scriptures. And just as plainly there is an old covenant or message remaining in the New Testament—namely, that conception and practice of religion based upon divine law against which the apostle Paul so vigorously contends. A theologian must be sensitive to the old within the new and the new within the old, so that when he speaks of continuity he will also not forget obvious discontinuity.

The balance necessary here may be suggested through the following incident. Several years ago a Welsh preacher was speaking at an American theological seminary on the theme of new life in

Christ. He painted the contrast in a man's life before and after his conversion in the boldest possible colors. Somewhat carried away by his subject, he declared that between the old man and the new there is absolutely not the slightest connection, that they have nothing to do with one another at all. After the service was over, a retired professor as he left the building was heard to mutter, "No connection at all, except that they're the same man."

Do we not face a similar complexity in Christian biblical interpretation? If the New Testament is simply the Old over again, then nothing has really happened in Jesus Christ to change man's existence under God. But if the two Testaments are utterly distinct in theological perspective, then nothing has happened either. One may safely venture the prediction that theological work in the next decade will turn again to the discontinuities which qualify the biblical continuity, and to the variety which enters into the making·of the biblical unity. The other side of the truth has been ably presented and well learned.

A second theme stressed in recent biblical theology is that of the divine-human encounter. "In both Testaments, then," writes C. H. Dodd, "everything turns upon an encounter of man with God."[1] The narratives and prophecies, commandments and visions which together make up the literary and theological substance of the Bible are accordingly treated as illustrations of the central, unifying encounter motif. However the relationship of God to man is pictured, whether as king-subject, master-slave, husband-wife, or father-son, encounter remains central and constant. All these and other instances of encounter, it is pointed out, counterbalance elements of distinctness and otherness by elements of reciprocity and fellowship, although never in such a way that the basic asymmetrical relation of divine independence and human dependence is destroyed.

Perhaps it is noteworthy that the encounter motif should seem most controlling in the books of the Old Testament, where again it is most pertinent in expounding passages of the prophetic type in which features of surprise, besetment, or even conflict are likely to be prominent. The situation thus conveyed is chiefly one of "challenge-and-response," to borrow Toynbee's well-known

[1] C. H. Dodd, *The Bible Today* (Cambridge: Cambridge University Press, 1952), p. 104.

phrase. There is God's action and claim, in judgment and mercy, and here is man's responding, in freedom and faith.

We shall be thinking later in this chapter of the Word of God as a pattern of Christian interpretation; but let us simply point out here how closely it is tied to the conception of encounter. The Word chiefly designates a situation of being addressed and of answering; and back of "Word" lies, of course, the idea of "will" —first, God's will, acting upon man by addressing itself to him, and second, man's will, which is affected by being thus addressed whether it chooses to accept or refuse its true Lord. God's Word comes to men from beyond themselves, to quote Dodd once more, "as the interpretation of a situation, requiring action in that situation."[2]

There can be no doubt that the theme of encounter does run through the Bible and has signal importance for biblical exegesis. Yet there is a real question whether the recognition and tracing of this theme amounts to a profoundly *theological* achievement. Can "encounter" possibly bear the weight which has been assigned to it? For one thing, it seems much too rigid a term to cover the biblical richness of images like covenant, sacrifice, or marriage, which say all that "encounter" says, and more. For another, it seems far too empty a word experientially; in some cases at least it is rendered almost spatially as if it meant sheer up-againstness, mere contact and impact, or the intersection of two orders. But perhaps its greatest disadvantage for theology lies in the fact that it catches up little or no sense of the passage of time, as the setting forth of God's *Chesed* or steadfast love would certainly require. In short, what we have here is undoubtedly a necessary but rather minimal motif for biblical interpretation which cannot possibly, as is claimed, order and unify Scripture as a whole.[3]

The third emphasis in biblical theology is a drastically changed idea of history. When a theologian talks these days to a historian, one might expect them to agree at least on what the word "history" means. But they seldom do. I say, "Christianity is a historical faith." My historian friend immediately thinks of this in terms of records and other documents like memoirs or eyewitness

---

[2] *Ibid.*

[3] For a fuller treatment see my article, "Religion as Encounter," in *The Journal of Religious Thought*, Spring-Summer, 1957, pp. 129–39.

reports by which past events can be verified and reconstructed. This, however, is not what I have in mind at all. I mean, instead, that Christianity is a faith *about* history, as well as one having a historical origin and development. To call Christianity a historical faith is to declare that set down in the midst of historical happenings there are mighty, unmistakable clues to the meaning of history as a whole; it is, indeed, to refuse to separate entirely an event from its meaning, on the premise that the two are lived together and must therefore be understood together.

To be sure, the Christian thinker has a vast body of materials— letters, chronicles, and narratives, as well as less "reliable" documents such as visions, prophecies, or poetry—to which he may direct the historian's attention. Yet the two are bound to read this material differently. To the historian, it is useful insofar as it helps him to reconstruct the past "as it actually was"; to the theologian, on the other hand, it serves not a reconstructing but a *reconfirming* purpose; it does not so much inform as testify. The books of the New Testament, for example, supply really very little data concerning social and economic conditions in first-century Palestine, and one would be rather foolish to consult them primarily to discover these conditions. What they provide is certainly a record, but a record of a totally different kind—that of God's own deed and self-disclosure in the one whom faith calls Jesus Christ.

Can we then speak of the Bible as history at all? Is it not, rather, "Scripture," "Holy Writ," or "God's Word"? But all these terms include the idea of a record, *res scriptae*, which is at the basis of the very meaning of history of whatever sort. And farther back, these words for the Bible point to history in the primary sense, that of *res gestae*, human events themselves. When a theologian calls the Bible history, he is affirming the sheer *happenedness*, if this word be permitted, of what is recorded therein. His stress is not upon the accuracy of its information but upon the fidelity of its testimony. Yet this does not mean that the theologian is unconcerned with history in the historian's sense of the term, but only that he is unwilling to restrict or scale down the meaning of history to a bare factuality, although of course he cannot finally get along without employing history in this sense as well.

Biblical theology today is not as troubled as it ought to be by the fact that it generally uses history in a very special and indeed, as Richard R. Niebuhr remarks, a "non-historical" sense. The sharp lines that are drawn between secular and sacred history, the rendering of *Heilsgeschichte* or the history of salvation in terms of divine determination rather than human freedom, and the tendency to bracket or by-pass the "historical Jesus" in favor of the Christ of the church's faith—all these spell logical confusion and semantic isolation. About each of them a great deal might be written, but here we must be content to point out the simple fact that what most biblical theologians mean by history is just what historians themselves are wont to call myth, saga, or legend —almost the very opposite of history as they understand it. And this situation is hardly conducive to any fruitful conversation between faith and culture as represented by these two disciplines, which might seem to be close together but actually remain far apart.

I do not believe that this situation in biblical theology should be permitted to continue. The theological question about history cannot be answered by the bare assertion of God's mighty acts or by positing a special kind of "faith-event." At the same time the whole biblical conception of history as centered in Christ, who is prophesied and announced, who makes events meaningful and meanings eventful, must not be discarded. Can theology achieve a frankly Christian view of history in which the demands of historical accuracy and theological adequacy can both be met? Contemporary thinkers such as Butterfield, H. Richard Niebuhr, and Tillich have already made telling contributions to this end: but what is now required is a resolute facing of the meaning of history from both directions, with a mutual disposition toward understanding.

One thing which may help to overcome the present impasse is the growing conception of the Church as the community that *remembers* Jesus Christ. The stress in biblical theology upon the unity of Scripture has its counterpart in the present-day ecumenical insistence upon continuity or tradition in the household of faith. The Pauline image of the Church as the body of Christ has received new significance in our own time, particularly assisted by biblical studies in the "corporate personality" of Israel as the people of God. May there not, then, be a genuine sense in which all Christian history is actually memory, that is, a living and conscious linkage with our own past, rather than a reproduction or translation carried on at a great distance from the original, shaping events of the Church? An entire view of time is at issue here, to which we shall give our attention later in the chapter. Frontier movements in psychology and the social sciences, such as Jung's theory of the collective unconscious, are also important in this connection.

These three contemporary stresses in biblical theology, then, all need supplementing and correcting from their own and from other perspectives before the claims of Christian theology can be fully met. What has now become abundantly clear, I think, is that to take a biblical stand amounts to far more than simply taking a stand on the Bible. There is much careful work to be done at the systematic and apologetic levels in theology before the biblical beachhead already established can be broadened and deepened. This will take us well beyond the self-imposed boundaries of biblical theology in its present phase, into a theological terrain where both the risks and the rewards are greater.

II It is time to ask a question about this development called biblical theology. Some of us have had the uneasy feeling that however biblical it may be, the movement lacks decidedly in theological scope and force. The question which has been stirring in our minds may be stated rather simply and abruptly. Granted that Christian theology must always, among other things, be biblical interpretation, is it true that biblical interpretation is necessarily Christian theology? To be sure, no one proclaims in so many words that it is, but many speak and write as if they were assuming it. This assumption, when and if it is made, ought to be laid bare and challenged in the name of theology itself.

There are certain dangers involved in any kind of theologizing which purports to be entirely or exclusively biblical in its orientation and intent. One that is often mentioned is that of "sophisticated fundamentalism." Just what that charge means is not altogether clear, and the danger referred to may be more apparent than real. Surely the majority of people working in this field are sophisticated in the sense that they accept and indeed adopt critical methods of scientific inquiry in their study of the Bible.

They are not literalists, nor do they believe in scriptural inerrancy or infallibility. But as the saying goes today, they "have a problem," which I believe consists in thinking that schematic biblical interpretation can somehow take the place of systematic theological reflection. In fact, they seem to be working on the assumption that the Bible, if not a book of Christian doctrine, is at any rate a book which makes doctrine secondary and instrumental to its own elucidation.

The assumption that biblical interpretation makes systematic theological reflection unnecessary, or at least somewhat superfluous, is rapidly gaining ground among some teachers and many students in our seminaries. It should be pointed out, however, that this can only be assumed because the character of biblical interpretation itself has greatly changed within the last generation. Without abandoning the canons of historical and critical scholarship, present-day interpreters of Scripture emphasize even more the tracing of themes and motifs running through its parts and giving conceptual and symbolic unity to the whole. In other words, the Bible comes to have primary theological significance only because it is read theologically, that is, with an eye to recurring patterns of imagination and understanding found within it and made clues to its interpretation in the context of Christian faith. The point which now needs to be made is that one can find theological meaning in the Bible only if he brings theological perspective to the study of the Bible. True, such a perspective is encouraged and made imperative by the kind of book the Bible is, rather than being added to it or forced upon it. But for all that, the stress in biblical study today is as much theological as the accent in theology is biblical. This should be more generously admitted than it usually is.

The work of Karl Barth is particularly instructive here. In his *Church Dogmatics* biblical themes and theological categories are so closely intertwined that they easily tend to become confused with each other. Thus, for example, he regards the doctrine of the Virgin Birth, "the miracle of Christmas," as utterly essential for understanding the Incarnation, "the mystery of Christmas"; and he uses the parable of the prodigal son to elucidate the self-revealing deed of God in Jesus Christ. Much of his doctrinal writing is but scriptural paraphrase or repetition, a set of variations upon biblical themes and insights. But all this proceeds on the basis of a central, dominant theological principle, maintained throughout with logical strictness and definitional precision—namely, Barth's conception of the revealed and revealing Word of God, which does not cease to be God even as it assumes human flesh. It is perhaps impossible to say whether biblical or theological factors are the more controlling in Barth's thought; yet it is altogether clear that both are present and interpenetrating. For Barth, theology is not simply exegesis, nor is exegesis ever all that is meant by theology.

Nevertheless the impression persists that, given the community of Christian faith, the Bible contains within itself all that is needed for its own interpretation, which is almost if not quite to say that the Bible interprets itself. The fear that theologians may bring to bear a way of viewing which is "alien" or "foreign" to the Bible seems to be grounded in this impression. The only kind of theology allowable on such a basis is recital theology, a recounting of the mighty acts of God which is more like translation than interpretation. The retelling moves safely and securely inside the confines of the biblical framework; to step outside them would be regarded as a sort of treason.

By contrast with this safely biblical idea of theology, what usually is called systematic theology seems almost tentative and questioning. Most of what goes under the name of biblical theology today consist of declarative or imperative statements. It abounds in flat assertions, take-it-or-leave-it propositions, emphatic repetitions. One soon wearies of the very style of such writing. Even more, one misses the inquiring, exploring temper which belongs to genuine theological thought in our own or any age. Instead, one seems to have intruded upon the ideology of a community bent chiefly on protecting and preserving itself, like the Indian cliff dwellers of the Mesa Verde in Colorado or the monks of Qumran in the desert near the Dead Sea.

How different is the vigorous and independent work of a Tillich or, for that matter, a Barth! Like all truly creative Christian thinkers, these men do more than reminisce or restate the gospel; they rethink and in some sense actually relive it. They stand consciously, deliberately at the frontier between the church and the world, sometimes looking out and sometimes looking in, but always confronting not only fellow believers but fellow men and conveying the "lively oracles of God" to them. It has been said of Barth (by Gustav Wingren) that although he seems to be speaking of God he is really talking about man, and it might be said of Tillich that when he writes about man he is really thinking of God The point is that theological interpretation is essentially a kind of mediation. So far as the Bible is concerned, this involves not merely bringing its meaning to the reader but also bringing the existence of the reader to the Bible. One cannot take place, really without the other. Even if the gospel is to be "thrown like a stone" at contemporary man, it has to be aimed at its target and there may actually be something in the human situation today which requires and welcomes such paradoxical, peremptory treat ment. There are times when the best apologetics is polemics. But there are other times when we do well to examine carefully the ground we stand on and the distance from it to the places where other people—those for whom Christ also died—actually live Our time, I am convinced, is of this latter sort.

Here we come near to what Rudolf Bultmann has been telling us, that some way must be found to release the gospel from it biblical world-view so that it may find man where he now lives He asks a question which I think can be put rather simply: "Wha has happened to the gospel?" He asks the question sadly, but h insists upon asking it. And of course the answer which must b given is that we have obscured the gospel and need to recaptur it for men and women in our day.

How have we obscured the gospel? By insisting that it is al of a piece with the fashion and framework in which it is presented Bultmann asserts. In reaction against liberal theology, with it interest in discovering a universal and spiritual "essence" withi the changing thought-forms and outworn superstitions of th Bible, neo-orthodox theology has been stressing the unity o wholeness of the Bible; it has been somewhat perversely preo cupied with its "strangeness," its "uniqueness," its paradoxica "offense" to the modern intelligence. Doubtless this had to b to counteract the liberal stress upon accommodating and harmo izing; but counteraction is not enough. The danger now is tha Christians will say things in church which contradict what the believe everywhere else, that they will not distinguish betwee what is supremely important and what is frankly dispensable in the Bible, and that they will "swallow whole" its three-story universe, theories of demonic possession and angelic intervention, and all the rest as easily as they accept the heart of the Christian message. Bultmann thinks this danger can and must be avoided. If not, Christianity is likely to become no more than a cozy ritual of "togetherness," a mumbling of biblical noises, a mutual self-assurance.

I may have overstated the danger, but it is because I have seen how theological trends "filter down" through pastors, periodicals, and lesson books into the church at large. At all events I believe Bultmann has something very like this in mind. How does he propose to recapture the gospel? By his well-known program of "demythologizing." In one sense there is nothing new about this program, since every generation does its own demythologizing, if that means distinguishing between the Bible as a whole and the message or gospel which is central to it. But Bultmann means more than this; his concern is not so much with selectivity as with validity; he wishes us to face the question of the truth of the Bible. The gospel is to be recaptured by being set free from its setting in a world-view which is necessarily untrue for us because it is unscientific. And he proposes to bring this about, not by trying to establish some hard core of fact within the Bible (which he knows is impossible) but by extracting from the Bible a human situation that is strangely universal and constant, alongside a divine demand that is equally contemporaneous with every age.

This almost classic feature of biblical revelation-and-response, in which the will of God calls for man's decision and obedience, is what is left for Bultmann after the Bible has been demythologized. Certainly it is not a rational or moral essence that is here identified with the gospel. The question is, however, whether it is nonmythical. Has Bultmann perhaps only replaced an ancient mythology by a contemporary one? Would not remythologizing be a better word for what he proposes?

For all the many real and sharp differences between Bultmann and Barth, both men are plainly less biblical and more theological than is often supposed. Bultmann is obviously closer than Barth to philosophical categories and methods and is quite frank in acknowledging his indebtedness to Heidegger's existentialism for some fundamental insights. Barth, however, may be used to correct Bultmann at one important point, having to do with the indispensability of myth and symbolism in setting forth the Christian message. There is, says Barth, a very real sense in which you cannot separate the mythical from the nonmythical elements in Scripture without violating the unity of Scripture. For example, can the meaning of Jesus' parable of the good Samaritan ever be understood if the pictorial, story-like character is analyzed away until only a formal principle or classic situation is left? Clearly not, for as soon as the picture is compressed into a principle the truth of the picture is lost. This is what Jesus himself rebuked the lawyer for, who wanted a definition of the neighbor. Jesus gave him a picture of neighborly love instead. Only if we retain the symbolic and even legendary element in Scripture can we really have anything significant to do with Scripture, although we certainly should not leave this element unrecognized or presume to literalize it.

But the merit of Bultmann's viewpoint is the explicit way he declares that what gives unity to the Bible is its concern with the meaning of human existence in the light of God's kingly, saving act in Christ. This concern, he holds, is common to the document, the reader, and the interpreter, and makes possible their mutual involvement in the message of the Bible. Hence the interpreter is no translator but a mediator, capable of negotiating the historical and mythical distance between document and reader by virtue of his common involvement in both situation and message. Emphatically, this is not a one-sided process. The reader must be brought to the Bible as well as the Bible brought to the reader.

And surely it takes a theologian versed in Scripture, rather than a biblical scholar given to sketching out "themes" and "motifs," to bring them together. The Christian theologian necessarily faces two ways—toward the Bible, which records God's holy purpose and saving deed for us, and toward the world, where people actually live and which God so loved that he gave his Son to free mankind from sin and death and anxious guilt. In theology we read the Bible backward and forward from Christ, who stands not only in the middle of the Testaments but in the center of history itself. And only theology can thus interpret Scripture and contemporary man to each other—not, of course, because theologians are better or wiser than biblical scholars, but because theology has its own built-in safeguards against schematism, premature categorizing, ideological isolation and defensiveness. For, as Emil Brunner remarks somewhere in perhaps rather rueful vein, even theological thought is logical thought, which means that it is willingly subject to the rules of meaningful discourse, prominent among which are consistency of statement, objectivity of reference, and rational inference. It is the logic implicit in the theological task which keeps us from confusing symbol with system, image with category, or paradox with absolute truth.

If we are able to maintain Barth's emphasis upon the Christological center of the Bible, together with Bultmann's insistence upon the constant human situation to which God addresses his ultimate claim, then we may be on the way to recovering our sense of theological balance in the interpretation of Scripture. But beyond both Barth and Bultmann there remains, quite simply, the question of truth, which Heinrich Vogel rightly says is the only real issue in theology today. The task of theology, admittedly difficult, is to interpret the Bible backward and forward from Christ in such a way that the divine revelation uttered in him is communicated as saving truth to the minds and hearts of men.

III So we come to our next point. What is the relationship between revelation and communication, between God's self-disclosure in Jesus Christ and Christian discourse concerning it? The attempt to distinguish clearly between the Word of God and the words of men about it is an ancient and perennially necessary one. However, it is also exceedingly complicated and treacherous, since we do not have in our possession any simple rules for making such a distinction and must necessarily use human thought and language in attempting it. Although it is well that we should be warned not to confuse our words with God's own Word, it is quite another matter to draw a precise boundary line between the two. Furthermore, every genuine distinction presupposes also some relationship or likeness within which the distinction becomes possible and significant. This last point is all too often ignored in present-day discussion of this central issue.

By and large, what has been happening in recent biblical

theology is that God's revelation has been rendered chiefly in dynamic, active terms, while its interpretation has been conceived as part of the "response" of faith. The distinction, then, has been between God's deed in Christ and man's appropriation or reception of this deed in faith. Even where the phrase "Word of God" is used to denote revelation, in accordance with ancient biblical and doctrinal tradition, it customarily carries this dynamic stress, signifying not so much what God says as the act of God's speaking itself.

It is true that in Hebrew "word" retains the primitive, powerful sense of energy being put forth, of will expressing itself. For God, at least, to say is to do; divine speech is divine power. In Greek, however, *logos* conveys more the form or shape of what is spoken than the bare speaking itself. Used of revelation, it points us to the meaning and truth that is in Jesus Christ rather than to the sheer fact that he is the utterance of God. It is noteworthy that in recent biblical theology the Hebrew accent has tended to crowd out the Greek. Thus revelation has come to signify a divine action or event which forces its way into history and human consciousness, "intersecting" time, "confronting" men and women, and "demanding" the response of faith.

This whole way of speaking about revelation has indeed become so much a part of theological discussion that it is hard for us to see what a foreshortened and truncated view of God's Word it often presupposes. Yet already this is growing clearer, and one may safely predict that in the near theological future some conceptions which are so dominant will seem peculiarly dated and unfruitful. We shall then be ready for a more ample, spacious rendering of revelation, which does not forget Barth's warning that "God's language is God's mystery" but at the same time incorporates Tillich's view that *logos* is as much meaning as event, as much truth as deed of God.

The way will then be open to face the relationship between revelation and communication in a different, theologically far more adequate way. First of all, it may once again become plain that God's Word in Christ is not a sheer act contradicting all we know and interrupting the flow of rational discourse as a kind of cryptic cipher which only utterly obedient, unquestioning faith is able to read. The test of revelation, the only possible test, is simply that it *reveals*. But a "hole in history," as Barth calls the revelation in Christ, does not reveal anything. It is even a question whether in this viewpoint God even discloses himself to faith, since Barth keeps telling us that nothing new about God is learned, that God keeps his own secret even as he speaks.

On the contrary, must we not affirm that when God speaks he declares something about himself which casts an ultimate light upon the mystery of our existence and our salvation? In other words, is not revelation itself communication—to be sure, a unique and if you will privileged communication, but nevertheless meaningful and illuminating to man? Only on such terms as these can Christians make sense out of God's decisive deed in Jesus Christ, which can hardly be decisive if it is not also truly significant. Theology dominated by biblical symbols and so-called categories has been extremely chary of phrases such as "revealed truth" or "the meaning of revelation" for reasons which may formerly have been sufficient but are so no longer. This reluctance came out of theology's strong reaction against liberalism on the one hand, with its concern for intelligibility and reasonableness, and against fundamentalism on the other, with its interest in putting revelation into dogmatic propositions.

This reaction, while thoroughly understandable historically, does not have to be maintained indefinitely. Its benefits can be preserved without its more dubious exaggerations and distortions of the Christian message. It must now be said that revelation is God's own way of communicating with us, and that it indicates not only the fact that he speaks but the meaning and truth of what he says to us. Intelligence no less than impact, understanding no less than decision, belongs to what the Word implies. Hence Christian communication is bound up with revelation itself, is intended by it and continuous with it. "God has created man's mind intellectual, whereby we may take in his light," wrote Augustine. Just so; and the task of theology is not to show how revelation meets and fits man's mind, or how it contradicts and confounds man's mind, but how it both requires and remakes man's mind. Revelation is communication; and for making this clear, the Johannine and Augustinian image of light is surely much more pertinent and profound than the metaphors of impingement or challenge which have been greatly overdone of late. When Clement of

Alexandria wrote that the Word of God proceeds from the Father not like words from the mouth of a speaker but like a ray from a torch, a torch which is never extinguished, he pointed in the right direction. Revelation is not a bare act, and Christ is not a sheer event. In God's Word there is meaningful pattern and structure to be detected and pondered by the mind of man, which is made by God for saving knowledge of himself. This puts a rather different perspective on the whole matter than has been generally presented to us by theology in the recent past.

In the second place, regarding the connection between revelation and communication, it may now be seen that human words are not necessarily the confounding of the Word of God but may even be divinely purposed and inspired. They may be, in fact, revelatory of God. The whole doctrine of inspiration must be carefully reconsidered, but two things may be said about it initially. One is that the doctrine has been too exclusively tied to that of Scripture, as if all inspiration must be biblical. The other is that its relationship to the Christian understanding of the Holy Spirit has been far too automatically and impersonally conceived. Inspiration cannot be mechanical causation or external dictation; that would be the very opposite of what the word means. On both these points much work remains to be done.

The principle that human words may be revelatory of God, however, is not exhausted in the doctrine of inspiration. It looks in at least two further directions, which can be only briefly sketched here. One has to do with the current discussion going on around the Christian world regarding tradition and Scripture. The Mass is tradition, and so are the historic creeds, liturgies, and forms of church organization and discipline. In Protestantism we ordinarily try to set the Bible as God's Word over against all this historic development and to assert the primacy of Scripture over tradition both in time and in authority. Sometimes we even recall that the very word "tradition" has the same Latin root as the word *traditor*, "traitor," and we speak about the way in which no tradition can be sacrosanct because it alters, unconsciously perhaps but inevitably, the original form of the gospel.

Now this certainly cannot be denied. But what recent biblical scholarship has helped us all to see is that tradition, in the form of summaries of belief, acts of corporate worship, teaching devices, etc., is actually in the Bible and must be regarded in some sense as pre-biblical. Therefore, to set up Scripture as the superior judge of tradition is simply to fly in the face of what we already know to be true about the composition of the Bible and the growth of Christian traditions. Every so often Protestants need to be reminded that the Bible is a very human book—not simply the "record" of God's revelation, which is somehow "contained" in it, but the shaping and expressing of that revelation in communicable form. Such a reminder is the perennial service which biblical studies can render to theology.

Where does this leave us, then? In the Catholic position that tradition is and must be the trustworthy interpretation of Scripture? Hardly; but we should be able now to see the truth in that position as never before in Protestant theology, without capitulating to its excesses and papal rigidities. What is needed is the kind of interaction between Catholic and Protestant views which alone can correct blind spots and comprehend authentic differences. One hopes that in the ecumenical conversation which has barely begun between the sundered parts of Christendom, a conversation we shall be commenting upon in the next chapter, a more viable position can be found that will do justice to this whole issue. Suffice it to say here that biblicism is no antidote to traditionalism, and that as Protestants become more sensitive to the authentic Christian tradition persisting among a great variety of traditions they will surely grow more self-critical of their own biblical assertiveness.

The idea that biblical language is somehow closer to revelation than liturgical and doctrinal language does not stand up under critical scrutiny. If one means that the Bible "records" or "contains" revelation with a fidelity unmatched by the literature of Christian devotion, worship, or theology one is really on very shaky ground, especially when it is recalled that these latter elements go into the making of the Bible itself. Erich Auerbach in his important book *Mimesis* has carefully studied Christian style in contrast to classical and secular styles, rightly regarding Christian and biblical styles as one. He shows how St. Augustine, trained as he was in pagan rhetoric and steeped in classical literature, still remains faithful to biblical modes of thought and speech. Christian language *is* biblical language only because the

Bible is read, interpreted, and in part even composed in an unmis-
takably Christian fashion.

The matter we have been discussing has one further dimension
which will bear looking into. The relationship between divine
revelation and human communication may become still clearer
when we keep in mind that communication between men moves
on many different levels, serves different purposes, and uses different means. Therefore not all human words are at an equal
distance from the Word of God; some may well be more apt
vehicles than others for conveying Christ. The Bible itself, of
course, is a telling illustration. Narrative or recital is only a small
part of it, and not necessarily the most characteristic part. Oracles,
visions, poems, hymns, sermons, laws, and stories are its major
portion. What this means is that the message of God's saving deed
in Jesus Christ is not simply told and retold but responded to,
appropriated, wrestled with, bodied forth. Thus the unity of
Scripture is a unity-in-variety, in which a filament of historical
happenedness is interwoven with paeans of praise, anguished pray-
ers, ejaculations of doubt and revolt, and dramatic imaginings.

Hence biblical communication itself moves on suggestive, evoca-
tive, deliberately symbolic planes. If, as Hendrik Kraemer recom-
mends, we are to see Christian communication in biblical perspective, we shall realize that it requires a whole battery of approaches,
methods, and forms. In particular, the Bible is rich in what is
called today existential communication, the sort of writing which
does not present the reader with a *fait accompli*, even a divine
one, but seeks to reveal him to himself and bids him take part
in what is set forth. It does not put before him something to
which he can be indifferent but evokes and elicits his own involvement. Thus it aims at arousal, self-knowledge, possibly even
irritation, but always commitment and consent in the last analysis.
Pascal and Kierkegaard, who were deeply biblical in the tone and
intent of their style, were masters of this way of writing. Their
work moves us still because it was cast at the level not of recital
but of evocation. More than a declaration of faith, it was an
invitation to faith. That is the characteristic greatness of Christian
communication in every age, and it is founded firmly in the Bible
itself.

Such communication, whether or not it succeeds in revealing

God to men, does make possible what Berdyaev called "the reciprocal revelation of man in God." Perhaps the Bible itself can do no more than this. On its highest levels of poetic insight, spiritual discernment, and moral passion, communication and revelation almost seem to merge and interact. That is why it is truer to say that the Word of God, spoken in Christ, includes the Bible than to say that the Bible contains the Word of God. As if anything could contain him in whom all things cohere and have their primordial and final meaning! We must not claim for the Bible that which the Bible does not claim for itself, that which belongs solely to Christ as Lord.

It is then our faith in God's revelation in Christ that reads and judges Scripture, not Scripture that judges and reads faith, except in a secondary and derivative sense. Theologically, it would be still more valid to affirm that it is Christ who judges both our faith and Scripture, since he is the very power and wisdom of God disclosed for our redemption and renewal.

IV   Our last point has already been introduced in the preceding paragraphs, but it may be stated more precisely and completely here. The Christian doctrine of the Word of God is more than an explication of biblical revelation; it has also much to do with biblical interpretation. It has far wider, deeper bearings upon the whole range of Christian life and truth than are usually recognized today. Most important for our present concern is the freedom which this doctrine gives the theologian with respect to his interpretation of all that he has received from Scripture or tradition. It is not a counsel of safety, timidity, or prudence in interpretation, but one of daring, forthright, independent thought touching all Christian matters.

To be sure, as Barth and others have kept telling us, the reasons for this theological freedom are themselves thoroughly biblical reasons. Chapter and verse can be found for saying that the Bible has its own built-in provisions against biblicism, that is, against the refusal to interpret biblical meanings in any but biblical terms. This is true and needs to be said. But the provisions also need to be heeded and employed in theological interpretation, as well as merely granted. The reason we do not have to be bound down to the piecing together of biblical motifs and the transposition of these motifs into "categories" is that God has spoken to us his own Word about himself in Jesus Christ. We have this treasure in earthen vessels, of which the Bible is one—perhaps the chief one, but not the only one. Thus theologians have their own work to do even after exegesis and hermeneutics have been done. We have, in short, the task of understanding our faith and of understanding man, the world, and God in light of our faith, according to the principle that God has himself illumined all these things in speaking through his Son.

Here for example is the endlessly fascinating and perplexing doctrine of the trinity or three-in-oneness of God. Emil Brunner claims that the trinity is not a biblical doctrine at all but represents a concern for formulating and systematizing faith which is foreign to the Bible. The question we must ask Brunner, first of all, is whether any doctrine is biblical in the sense in which he wishes it to be. What in fact does it mean that a doctrine is biblical? Must it not mean that a doctrine taught by the church is founded in the Bible, suggested by it, perhaps made historically inevitable by it? All doctrines should have such a biblical basis, reasons for emerging in Christian history. Can it be doubted that the doctrine of the trinity has just this anchorage and impetus?

The idea widely shared especially among Christian laymen that the trinity is the last word in abstruse speculation, a kind of theological higher mathematics, is simply false. This is not to deny that it does tantalize and attract the most disciplined, sophisticated kinds of Christian intelligence, or that some formulations of the trinity have been disappointingly sterile and over-complicated. That must frankly be acknowledged. But it also must be seen that there had to be a doctrine of the trinity because of the utterly central Christian conviction that God has spoken anew in Christ a Word which he wants the whole world to hear and heed, a Word which does not abrogate so much as fulfill God's former revelation, a Word which must be taken seriously as the ultimate clue to what human existence under God ought to mean and be. As Karl Barth writes, the truth that God reveals himself a second time in Jesus Christ and that this truth is known through the imparting of God's spirit to men demands the doctrine of the trinity. God has more than one way of being God;

Father, Son, and Holy Spirit are our Christian way of saying so; and these terms are not arbitrary or "ideological" only, since they are required by the very nature of what happened to and for the world in Jesus Christ. They are also, of course, emphatically and wholly biblical, given Scripture for appropriation and reflection by our Christian understanding.

Therefore, it will not do to dispose of the trinity as an unbiblical doctrine, even in the yes-and-no fashion characteristic of Brunner. That this doctrine is indeed biblical in foundation and orientation, however, cannot be proved merely by exegesis, although exegesis will help, but requires also the disciplines of historical and systematic theology. It is by no means accidental that the classic creeds of Christendom are cast in trinitarian form; they had to be, because of the most intimate and persistent persuasions of what Schleiermacher called the Christian consciousness itself. The trinity is thus not a theological addition or elaboration but the very form of Christian interpretation, the very shape of our vision of the world, the very substance of our faith.

Or, to take another illustration, here is the conception of time which seems to be dominating the field of biblical theology at present. One can scarcely be grateful enough for the way in which our attention has been redirected to the whole eschatological dimension of our faith, with its undoubtedly important stress upon the "lastness of all things," the ultimate and indeed final significance of every choice for or against God made in every present moment. Nevertheless, some curious and contradictory statements about time are constantly being made, supposedly on behalf of the biblical and Christian view in contrast to other views of time. One must ask whether the biblical and Christian view is actually so (paradoxically) different from all other views, and whether it is best seen as a kind of standing, stubborn contradiction to them.

This question comes especially to mind in thinking of some recent attacks made on the Greek view of time by biblically conscious theologians. We are told that there can be nothing in common between the classical or cyclical way of regarding time and the biblical way. This is but the latest phase in that Christian reaction to and rejection of classical culture which was begun by church fathers like Tertullian and continued more recently by theological scholars under the strong influence of Adolf von Harnack.

There are two rather basic questions to be asked of those who would set off thus sharply Christian thinking about time from other ways of viewing it. One is whether the Christian view is simply the Hebrew view over again, so that the "Christ-event" simply fits into the prior framework already provided within the Old Testament, rather than "the reconciliation of Jew and Greek," as we followed P. T. Forsyth in saying in the first chapter. I shall not attempt to conceal my own strong preference for the latter position, which I believe does not so much abandon Jewish modes of thought as add to them the tremendous conviction of the eternity of God transcending and yet interpenetrating historical and natural time, thus redeeming time as men know and live it. The Jewish mind evidently had no conception of eternity in the Platonic sense, but the Christian idea of the Word of God as eternal surely seems to introduce the Platonic dimension into the doctrines of creation, revelation, and incarnation. This may not be "biblical," but it is in the Bible! And such a view of eternity, and of time as the "moving image of eternity," in Plato's words, is so indispensable to the interpretation of these doctrines that no amount of word study concentrating upon Hebrew terms can reduce or eliminate it from the Christian reading of Scripture. Let us remark, parenthetically, that word study is a very limited approach to doctrinal issues and seldom settles theological questions with finality, though of course it must be listened to and learned from at every possible point.

The other question to be asked is whether the consciousness and meaning of time characteristic of the Bible is really so unlike the general human experience and reflection of various cultures that it must be set against them conceptually and categorically. Have Bergson or Proust nothing of significance and validity to say to Christian thinkers about time? Must Augustine be rejected out of hand as making an illegitimate synthesis of biblical and classical elements in his view of time (or love, or man, or God)? It is certainly hard to believe that this is so, and on decidedly Christian grounds at that. We cannot believe that the Word of God addresses itself to human history, becomes an event in time, without understanding what time means to those who endure and exist in it. "Only through time, time is conquered," as T. S. Eliot writes in his *Four Quartets*.

About all this much more might be written, but here our interest must confine itself to affirming the need for illumination on the mystery of time from sources outside the Bible, as well as for a more generous and less schematic rendering of biblical views of time and eternity. By virtue of our faith in the eternal Word of God made flesh in Jesus Christ, we are as Christian thinkers free to explore this mystery in any and all directions, to attempt to say as best we can with help from every possible quarter just what it means, and to develop ways of interpreting history and eschatology which may claim not only biblical but general human validity and relevance. In particular, we may learn liberally from the poets and the philosophers who have been preoccupied with time. For our faith is that God's Word spoken in Christ is not merely a paradoxical impingement of eternity upon time but an entering into time that time may be redeemed from insignificance—the boredom of mere recurrence, the triviality of the "specious present," the vanity and evanescence of bare change. Our faith is that the eternal Word of God comes down into our time and, by the same token of the Incarnation, takes our time up into himself.

This says as much about history as about eternity, as much about man as about God. If we mean it when we declare that the incarnation of the Word is in very truth the clue to the significance of our time-bound existence upon earth, then nothing human can be foreign to it. And we who believe this do not need to develop further refinements in the special biblical language which we have been relearning; we need pre-eminently to become again adept in a more general human language which can portray and evoke the felt substance of experience all of us share under God.

To the trinity and time, as matters of Christian importance with which biblical theology has not dealt adequately, must be added the Holy Spirit. Here again a deliberately limited perspective, in part corrected by some excellent doctrinal studies with a more spacious outlook, has failed to give due theological weight to the Spirit. One of the surest and most necessary of the new accents in theology, therefore, is a stress upon the so-called "subjective" or experiential aspects of our Christian faith which have been distorted or neglected in recent years.

God is Spirit and man is spirit. Thus a kind of common ground is established between God and man, established moreover by God himself, bridging the "infinite qualitative distance" by a span that is anchored deeply in the nature of both. Yet this common ground is also an uncommon ground, since it lifts man above all to which he is related beneath him and opens man to all to which he is related above him. In terms of the doctrine of the Holy Spirit God not only addresses himself but makes himself available to man. As in Christ he binds himself to us so also he releases and imparts through Christ his own unbounded, unutterable energy of being. We may insist that it is by means of God's Word that we know his Spirit, but it is just as true to say that it is through his Spirit that we hear and heed his Word.

According to this doctrine man, however deeply mired in sin, is nevertheless capable of answering and witnessing to God's Spirit by virtue of the spiritual nature which God has imparted to him. Above all else the gift of the Spirit to man is fellowship or communion with God. In Christ we have opened up to us not a way of relationship based on response but a way of reunion based on a bestowed participation in the mystery of the divine life. This is a far bolder and more daring affirmation than we are likely to hear today, except from thinkers closer to the great ancient tradition like Berdyaev or Tillich; but who can doubt that it is an authentic, indispensable affirmation?

Indeed, one may develop with the help of the doctrine of the Holy Spirit an entire theological understanding which may be quite at variance with that of the last generation, which was rightly called a theology of the Word. As the Word is the principle of particularity and God's self-definition, so the Spirit is the principle of universality and God's self-impartation and diffusion. As P. T. Forsyth saw half a century ago, these principles lead theologically in different directions touching the nature of the church; they also differ markedly in their renderings of the meaning of Christian experience, worship, and theology itself. But the important thing is that the principles should be kept and thought together within the trinitarian framework of theological interpretation. They are not antithetical but complementary, mutually involved, and in the last analysis theologically inseparable.

There can be no question, however, that at the present moment we should place our accent on the principle of the Spirit, with all that it implies for church order and worship, the ministry, and missions, as well as for the life of Christians in the wider world of nature and culture. Theology has proved, again and again, its inability to grasp and voice all Christian truth at once. It must content itself with making partial statements, true under the conditions and for the purposes for which they are made, but not claiming to embrace the whole gospel or the final truth. Granting this, our accent in the time immediately ahead must clearly be upon the Holy Spirit, not so much as a theological *leitmotif* but rather as an angle of theological vision which, properly and wisely used, can temporarily redress the balance that is in danger of becoming lost.

In the light of this new accent the meaning of St. Paul's rule that spiritual things must be interpreted spiritually will again become plain. The underlying affinity between man's search for ultimate reality and his response to revelation as conveyed in the Bible will be seen and set forth. We shall understand that since in faith we have to do with God as Spirit, he will by his very nature escape the fragile net of words we try to throw around him, breaking open even his own Word to us for our good and for his glory. Thus we shall be enabled to add to God's own work of making the Word become flesh our profoundly human task of making flesh become the Word.

Theology as Consensus

> The one Christ has made his Church one.
> —John A. F. Gregg

I   Present-day theology proceeds for the most part on the ecumenical level and devotes itself to truly ecumenical matters. More and more, it represents and fosters a concern of the whole church for its work and witness in the world. Less and less does it move in restricted denominational circles or seek to justify denominational differences. Naturally some groupings in the Christian community have moved farther in this direction than others, but all are becoming clearer as to the ecumenical character and purpose of theology itself.

Even this late in the day, however, it may not be amiss to take a fresh and careful look at the word "ecumenical." We need to be reminded just what it does and does not mean, if only because it is bandied about so freely. I once preached a sermon in a small New England village during which I had a great deal to say about ecumenical things. Afterwards, at dinner, my hostess asked me to repeat the word I had used so often and then, like a child with a new toy, kept trying it out with indiscriminate enthusiasm. She applied it to the taste of coffee, her great-grandfather's portrait, and the view of the lake from her porch. She thus gave the preacher an elementary lesson in the principles of communication.

There is some tendency in our churches to use "ecumenical" with similar enthusiastic vagueness and semantic irresponsibility. Take, for example, the rather general habit of employing it as a synonym for "interdenominational." The justification for this practice is that in our denominationally structured American Protestantism it is very difficult, if not impossible, for any one denomination to incorporate and demonstrate the wholeness of the church of Christ. For one thing, its memory is too short, seldom going back beyond the time of its own founding fathers except perhaps to jump with seven-league boots over fifteen centuries or more to what is taken to be primitive Christianity. This does not make for the sort of hospitality toward modes of thought and life other than one's own which is, after all, a *sine qua non* of ecumenical endeavor.

It is important, therefore, that we should try to correct our narrow, nearsighted outlook by engaging in various kinds of interdenominational activity, becoming acquainted with other forms of Christian life and work, faith and order than those we know best, and wherever possible joining with other churches in common discussion and enterprise. For it is clearly the case that in our denominationally oriented situation no one church can be the whole church or even fairly represent that wholeness. Each requires the other for realizing what the word "church" means, so that in this sense "ecumenical" is bound to signify "interdenominational" in current Christian discussion and action.

Yet it is every bit as plain that no amount of mere "getting together" can ever guarantee authentic ecumenicity. The best illustration of this fact is probably the so-called union service in which all the Protestant ministers in the community take part, demonstrating by their very presence on the platform and far more eloquently than anything which could be said to the contrary the divisive brokenness of contemporary church life. In such a setting any verbal tributes to church unity which might be paid are bound to ring rather hollow. Ecumenicity is emphatically not the necessary product of organizational mergers, world-wide contacts, letterhead changes, or church meetings on the grand scale. These things may be inspired by ecumenicity but they cannot assure it. Too often, indeed, they only succeed in producing a kind of ecumenical illusion which is a very poor substitute for the genuine article. Still, these institutional adjustments do make possible real encounter and exchange between the members of various ecclesiastical bodies; they facilitate cooperation; and they keep alive the recognition that there is a unity deeper and truer than our differences and divisions.

So long as "church" continues to mean "denomination" in the American scene, there will be a real need for interdenominational cooperation on as many fronts as possible. The danger is that this will be regarded as itself ecumenical when as a matter of fact it may threaten such real ecumenicity as we have, since of course interdenominationalism presupposes the denominational form and view of the church itself. There is thus an ambiguity, not to mention a paradox, implicit in any effort to identify the words "ecumenical" and "interdenominational." The theological reasons for this state of affairs will concern us later in the chapter.

A second common error in our present thinking, which persists among laymen and ministers despite much writing and teaching to the contrary, is that which equates ecumenicity with bigness. Thus people continue to speak of something called the ecumenical church, meaning by it the wider grouping or association of denominational representatives on a national or preferably a world scale which usually goes under the name of "council of churches." It is as if ecumenicity were to be arrived at by a process of addition and superimposition—an assumption which is thoroughly fallacious. The reasons for making it are not theological but cultural. They proceed not from a Christian understanding of the nature of the church but from our contemporary preference for massive organization and monolithic structure. Repeated warnings that the World Council of Churches, for example, has no ambition to become a super-church do not materially affect the average layman's view of ecumenical matters, which are seen in light of the same drive toward bigness manifested in other developments in business, industry, or political life.

To be sure, there is a kind of large-scale effort and wide-ranging vision which belongs to the essence of the ecumenical movement. In recent literature the close connection between the church's unity and the church's mission is frequently and properly stressed. Both have to be expressed and implemented in global terms if they are to become manifest at all. But this is always more a matter of scope than of mere size, and no good can come of confusing the two, as Christian people all too often do.

In answer to this prevalent notion, what has to be pointed out is that oneness, not bigness, is the true index of ecumenicity within the Christian church. While we may produce the latter by our own efforts, the former cannot be so produced. Our oneness is given to us by the very fact that we are Christians; it is we who belong to the church and not the church which belongs to us. Or, to put it just a bit differently, our oneness is not something which we Christians make, but something which makes us Christians. From this it follows that our ecumenical task today is not that of bringing Christian unity into being, but rather that of experiencing and expressing the reality in our midst which already makes us one in Christ. To be sure, better ways of doing this can and should be found, and yet the strong conviction that our oneness is given to us, not constructed by us, is the very center of the ecumenical vision and resolve in our own day.

Perhaps now we are ready to venture a definition of the word "ecumenical" which may commend itself to study and use at the "grass roots" level of the church's life and thought. The church, any and every form of church, is by its nature ecumenical, which means that it both reflects and requires the unity bestowed upon it by its Lord. Ecumenicity has to do with oneness in the sense of St. Augustine's saying: "We are Christians, we belong to Christ." Hence a hymn or prayer or deed of service is inherently and inescapably ecumenical, no matter how local or personal it may also be; and denominational efforts are no less ecumenical by nature than those of interdenominational agencies and assemblies. They cease to be ecumenical in their function only when they vitiate or deny the unity in Christ which by their nature they are intended to declare and demonstrate. The part must not presume to be the whole, and yet the part may validly and effectively represent the whole.

Oneness and wholeness, then, are the marks of what is ecumenical in the church. Both the local and the universal church are encompassed by the meaning of this word. One might even say that it refers to the local, "gathered" sense of the church within the universal church, and to the universal "notes" of the church made manifest to some degree in every neighborhood congregation.

For ecumenicity has to do with every part and function of the church, indeed with the very reality of the church. The clue to this idea is not sociological or psychological, but theological. That is to say that the church is one and whole by virtue of its living relationship to Christ the Lord, as shown in the great ecumenical images of the body and its members and the vine and its branches, given in the New Testament.

Before coming to the theological foundations of the ecumenical idea, there are some developments currently going on in our country which may be mentioned to make easier our grasp of this idea. One such development is the rapid growth of councils of churches, chiefly in metropolitan areas. We now have over five thousand such councils in the United States. This means that in American Protestantism we are making our decisions and taking action more and more co-operatively, on the basis of principles agreed upon and practices approved by representatives of churches within the community. Things are not so likely to be done in a corner or in the spirit of denominational rivalry. In the local council of churches the denominations are by no means overcome, but the basis of co-operation is the community rather than the denomination. Hence the denominational factor does not bulk as large as it does in the national and world councils of churches and is less a threat to the expression of the ecumenical reality of the church.

Several things may be noticed in connection with this development. One is that although local councils are assuming greater importance in many communities they still do not have enough power and authority to speak for all the Christians in these communities a relevant and significant word to contemporary situations. Hence they generally confine themselves to matters such as bingo playing, tavern licensing, or Sabbath observance on which agreement is rather easily secured, but which do not cut too deeply into the fabric of community life. In some cases, to be sure, the councils have done more than protest or exert pressure; they have set up counseling services and sponsored chaplaincies, provided study groups and educational ventures. But they generally lack the power to act decisively for their several churches on fundamental social issues, and so restrict themselves to symptomatic problems.

Another observation is that such councils move chiefly in the realm of strategy and planning rather than in that of Christian participation and purpose. They have not yet, by and large, faced squarely their own internal difficulties growing out of the pervasive denominational pattern. Their activism, strangely enough, is often a kind of escapism which avoids frankly ecclesiastical and theological concerns. It is always easier to denounce race-track gambling than to confess one's own infidelities and treacheries to the gospel. There are signs that these deeper notes are being struck, but the councils are still more community councils than church councils. They are more alert to the perils of the world outside the church than to those which fester within the church. If they were as truly ecumenical as they are pragmatic and programmatic, this would not be the case.

Yet the emergence of the councils may serve a significant ecumenical purpose if the consensus that is shaping up in practical affairs can be deepened to include concern for what makes the church the church and motivates its mission and witness in today's world. We have gotten together, we are talking together, we are working together. But are we growing together? Only time will tell.

A second thing is happening in American Protestantism which makes it easier for us to grasp what ecumenicity actually means. This is the return of the parish idea of the church, which has tremendous implications for our understanding of its nature as a household of faith. The construction of great tracts of housing near industrial centers, to which come people out of every conceivable religious background, has made possible again the conception of the parish as a piece of the world for which the church has definite Christian responsibility and stewardship. Sooner or later in such a sea of houses a church is set down. It may be Presbyterian, Methodist, Lutheran, Congregational, or possibly a "community church" (community churches are now becoming, oddly enough, a denomination of their own). By a series of rather complicated arrangements with other denominations, this denominational church becomes the church of Christ in that place. Although it is a part of some denominational structure or other, it is made up of members from a wide diversity of allegiance and background who are bound into it by the sheer physical fact of living in the same neighborhood.

It has been a long time since a local, denominational church has thus been regarded as the outcropping of the church universal in that place and has been given a slice of the world, so to speak, to cultivate and present to God. The older pattern of such churches existing side by side in the same neighborhood, imposing their religious divisions upon the community and competing with each other for support, is seriously shaken by this whole development. Furthermore, the parish idea of the church goes deeply against the grain of sectarian Protestantism as it has arisen in this country. But there is surely something in this emerging idea which is very positively related to more ancient and perhaps generic views of the reality of the church. The famous distinction made by Ernst Troeltsch between the "sect-type" and the "church-type" has received new documentation in our day, while at the same time becoming more difficult to maintain in practice.

There is an undoubted danger in this development which needs to be watched carefully and wherever possible avoided. As the parish churches lose their traditional and historic identity—their theological, liturgical, and behavioral uniqueness—they seem to be acquiring a kind of amalgamated character which is often more cultural than Christian, more American than ecumenical. As it becomes harder to tell a Methodist from a Presbyterian church, so it becomes harder to distinguish the church from the world. Must not the parish church, therefore, seek to become more fully and flexibly that which it really is, the church of Christ in that particular spot? Should it not, in its manner of work and worship, study and service, manifest more accurately and adequately its Christian reason for existence?

All this is by way of pointing out that there is an ecumenical paradox and an ecumenical anguish in our time. It is increasingly hard to find anyone who will approve and defend denominationalism as a form of Christian churchmanship, but everyone knows that he has to work within denominationalism. Even a parish church is denominationally supported and conceived, and can exist at present only through a series of comity arrangements engineered between denominational authorities and agencies. The ecumenical paradox is that although denominations are as yet the major way in which the institutional tasks of the church must be carried on, they are challenged and in principle denied by the very nature of the task to which they have been called. And the ecumenical anguish is that in our church life we need to find our identity as well as our inclusion and acceptance, so that we may know not merely that we "belong" but who we are and what we have to do as Christians under God.

The denominations, then, are like the broken symbols of which we spoke in our first chapter. They have always to be broken if they are to become pliable to the purposes of God for our own time and place. But they cannot be simply rejected or supplanted; they must be inclusively transcended, that the power and wisdom of God in Christ may move and work through them.

II   Now what is the task and role of theology in this changing situation and viewpoint? It can safely be laid down at the outset that theology has for the most part burst its denominational bonds. Actually there can no more be a denominational theology than a denominational hymnbook. True, it is denominations which publish hymnbooks, but hymnody itself is not denominational. And denominations still support theological seminaries, but the theology that is taught in them is less and less of a strictly denominational sort. Theology, like hymnody, is essentially and necessarily ecumenical; it cannot be made to serve a denominational turn without becoming special pleading or propaganda, rather than Christian inquiry into truth.

We do our theological work in this country chiefly through teaching, writing, and group study and discussion, spending therefore much of our time in face-to-face relationships that cut quite sharply across denominatonal lines. Where denominations form theological commissions it is not for the purpose of self-justification but in order to take fuller part in ecumenical discussion. One finds repeatedly that the deepest theological disagreements are likely to be those between members of one denomination rather than different denominations. Likewise, our greatest theological affinities are found across these same lines. Today, when a person describes himself as a high-church Baptist you do not smile as you would have done a decade ago; you know just what he means and where in the ecumenical spectrum he belongs. All this is by way of showing that strictly denominational theology scarcely exists today, except in some defensive backwaters of sectarian modes of thought, whether Protestant or Catholic.

Instead of denominational types of theology, we have a whole range of stresses and approaches running through most of the denominations. Some are tied more closely to a particular institution than others, of course. Thus there is an official Roman Catholic position on most doctrinal matters, laid down by popes and councils through the centuries. However, this is not confined to the church of Rome; it is shared in considerable degree by Orthodox theologians and by some Anglicans. But Protestantism itself has felt the influence of the catholic conception of the church, especially under the pressures growing out of the ecumenical movement, although Marian theology and the veneration of the saints have understandably not been able to draw Protestant support except in very rare instances. Anglican theology shows a remarkable consistency of outlook and is undoubtedly institutionalized to a large degree; but Anglicans are divided down the middle on some central issues, especially those regarding the liturgy.

On the Protestant side, the situation is even more complex. Fundamentalists who base their position on the sufficiency and infallibility of Scripture, conservatives who take their stand on certain cherished doctrines like the Virgin Birth or original sin in the sense of total depravity, liberals who maintain in some form the reasonableness of Christianity and the worth of the free human being before God, radicals who deny all centralized ecclesiastical authority and wish to rebuild the church on the simple model of a New Testament fellowship—all these are Protestant, but their greatest differences are among themselves. In some respects the fundamentalists are closer to the Roman Catholics than to other Protestants; and it is a fair question whether the humanist wing of Unitarianism should be termed Christian at all, let alone Protestant.

This naturally means that different pictures will be given of the theological situation depending upon what is taken as the set of issues provoking discussion and what standards of truth and relevance are to be applied to them. Actually, many kinds of theological spectrum can be devised for as many different purposes. One cannot, for example, discover today as neat and definite a line-up as that which church historians construct of the theological parties at the Council of Nicaea. The great doctrinal options still persist and are amply represented in contemporary Christian thought. It is even possible to classify theologians as modalist or monarchian, adoptionist or patripassianist; but this has dubious value except in reference to a particular issue, and the lines must be redrawn when others are to be considered.

At any rate, we find we have to use the words "protestant" and "catholic" in a theological as well as an ecclesiastical sense, and the theological sense cuts across the ecclesiastical. Thanks to the movement called neo-orthodoxy, contemporary Protestantism has acquired a theological perspective comparable in range and depth to that of historic Catholicism. Not even the fundamentalist groups are untouched by neo-orthodox influences, although they are prone to adapt and thus distort these influences for purposes of their own. The catholic and protestant tendencies show themselves in discussion of Scripture and tradition, the sacraments, Jesus Christ, social action and responsibility, as in the doctrine of the church. The former tendency emphasizes the historic continuity and authority of Christian institutions as God-given and God-directed; the latter stresses the sovereignty and transcendence of God above all visible and historic church life. One may roughly say that whereas the protestant tendency is prophetic, the catholic is sacramental; or that the difference is essentially between a view in which man is related savingly to Christ through the church and one in which man is related savingly to the church through personal faith in Christ. It is clear, furthermore, that within the ecumenical movement these tendencies are growing closer together and are gaining in mutual understanding and respect.

This gravitation, so to speak, toward the protestant and catholic poles may take place within a single denomination or, for that matter, a single individual. It is one of the results of the ecumenical movement that the claims and values of both poles should be more readily seen and appropriated. Thus a theological tension is set up which may be, in less stable minds, a mere oscillation back and forth between the poles; but when this tension is more fully entered into and thought through it may become the threshold of a truly ecumenical theology.

This double movement, which almost constitutes a sort of ecumenical rhythm, can be detected in the two questions which every theologian who is involved in ecumenical affairs must ask. The first is a question about traditions other than one's own within Christendom. The second is a question regarding the theologian's personal allegiance to a particular institutional form of Christianity.

The first question arises naturally in the wish to understand better the variety of forms of worship, doctrine, and polity which are brought together in any typical ecumenical conference. Here the Christian world is spread out in miniature, symbolized by different languages, costumes, kinds of ministry, and conceptions of the church. One sits down, for example, with a fellow delegate from the Mar Thoma church in India and asks him about his heritage, beliefs, and customs. There is a natural eagerness to learn as much as possible about the other, and a willingness to grant him his place in the church universal. The danger at this first stage of an ecumenical conversation, of course, is that of mere exoticism, fed by simple curiosity and love of the bizarre in Christian dress or opinion. This is a poor substitute for real charity of outlook toward each other. Yet the sheer awareness of the many-faceted, many-textured kinds of Christian life and thought in the world, rendered possible now as perhaps never before by the ecumenical movement, is an important first step in arriving at theological ecumenicity.

The second question is a reflex of the first. I cannot ask a fellow Christian about his form of faith without in turn being questioned about my own; and I am driven back to a deepened interest in the tradition which I represent. This has been the unexpected result of many conversations carried on under ecumenical auspices. People who had either taken denominational Christianity quite for granted or thought themselves superior to it have had to take it with unwonted seriousness. Hence a renewed or novel sense of historic particularity goes hand in hand with exposure to the more embracing reality of the church universal. The question "Who are you?" calls forth inevitably the question "Who then am I?" And both must be asked and answered ecumenically, charitably, by each party in the dialogue which is taking place. This may happen superficially, as the listing of differences and contrasts; but it may also happen at a more profound level, at which surprising basic affinities begin to appear. Paradoxically perhaps, but genuinely, we become conscious of our Christian unity not merely in spite of difference but through difference and possibly even because of difference. If no church in our time can presume to be the whole church, then it is also true that every church can and does disclose some precious facet of that wholeness which, apart from its own witness, would go disregarded and unseen.

Still another general comment should be made concerning ecumenical theology today. It is losing its highly individual and systematic orientation, becoming more and more representative in character. This does not mean that it is narrowly ideological or partisan, motivated by denominational self-justification; quite the contrary. Although theologians who attend ecumenical meetings realize that they are bound to speak for the churches which have sent them, they also realize that this is not the end of the matter but only the beginning. The roots of one's own tradition in the church are deeply intertwined with those of other traditions, so that what is most distinctive may be also what is most ecumenical as well. Indeed, it is the very uniqueness of our Christian witness that has universal import and implication for the whole church. In a real sense, then, theology is representative of the universal, ecumenical dimension of Christian truth since it is finally responsible to it.

Some consequences of such representativeness have, I think, proved unfortunate. Confronted by other theologians in an ecumenical gathering, one tends to speak cautiously, carefully, and with excessive politeness. Is this the kind of thing an Episcopalian ought to be saying? How will it sound to a Lutheran or a Baptist? Thus there comes into vogue what may be called an ecumenical style, even an ecumenical jargon, which is somewhat colorless and ponderous. It is, to be sure, an eminently churchly style, patterned closely upon biblical and liturgical phrasing and staying comfortably within the traditional framework of images and ideas. However, one does miss the inquiring boldness and creative tang of germinal theological thought; and one resents a bit the anonymous, declarative, and committee-produced quality of ecumenical statements.

On the other hand, there are some advantages to this way of putting things theologically. It is good for theologians to keep their ears to the ground, to keep in closer touch with the churches from which they come, and to feel that they must speak with a responsible voice. Too often in the past theologians have thought and written about the church without maintaining anything but a perfunctory relationship to any actual church organization. This individualistic character was one of the chief negative marks of the liberal theology of a generation or two ago, and it is good that it should have been challenged and in large part overcome in the so-called neo-orthodox theology. The dangers involved in "taking a Christian line" or remaining deliberately within the "circle of faith," while very real, are not the only dangers threatening the theologian. He must also avoid those of lofty condescension and irrelevance with respect to the actual forms and forces of the Christian enterprise in his own time and place.

The question, after all, is this: Just who or what does the Christian theologian represent? Have we now reached a stage in which he can do his thinking on behalf of the whole church of Christ? One hopes that the answer may be in the affirmative. At all events, thanks largely to the ecumenical movement, we are conceiving theology more and more in terms of a consensus—literally, a feeling together, growing together, thinking together about the things that are commonly believed among Christian people around the world. This is a conception of theology which may indeed push us beyond the present phase into a more assured, less defensive one in which denominational inhibitions will be exchanged for ecumenical freedom and amplitude.

III   So we come to our third topic: the search for theological consensus. Thus far we have been content mainly to discover areas of doctrinal agreement among theologians of diverse Christian backgrounds, specified against other areas of "unresolved differences" which require further study and discussion. The papers included in the volumes published in connection with the Lund Conference on Faith and Order illustrate this method. So too does Professor Walter Marshall Horton's book *Christian Theology: An Ecumenical Approach*.[1] This may with some truth be

[1] New York: Harper & Brothers, 1955.

termed the American way of coming at theological issues directly, in contrast to the more devious Continental way. It will be worth while to dwell a bit upon Professor Horton's version of it, together with some questions which it raises for us.

We Americans are a problem-solving people. We like to tackle issues in a blunt and forthright manner, talking them out, exposing them frankly, and reducing them to clear verbal outlines. Our faith in honest discussion is moreover matched by a similar confidence in the power of transparent good will to resolve difficulties. Professor Horton's book is thoroughly American in this amiable, disarming sense. He is able to build up a sanguine, hopeful case for ecumenical theology first by spelling out the points on which agreement has been or is being reached, then by listing the remaining differences with the implication that these may be removed in time by further discussion and a greater exercise of sympathy and patience. Some differences are naturally much harder to resolve than others, but the same agreement-seeking method of discussion can be depended upon to achieve resolution finally, surely, and happily.[2]

This whole outlook and procedure may appear so much a part of our American Christian pattern that it would seem ungrateful to call it into question. If in these matters we cannot take for granted the methods used in reasonable discussion, where can we put our trust? Nevertheless, there are deficiencies in such an approach which must be self-critically pointed out. We have now come to the place where it must be candidly asked, "Does consensus mean agreement?" There is considerable ecumenical evidence that such is not necessarily the case.

One way of getting at the question is to notice that agreement to use certain terms in common often hides real theological difficulties rather than revealing unity of thought. Thus it is quite possible for Quakers and Greek Orthodox, in conference assembled, to agree that they believe in the Real Presence or the indwelling Holy Spirit; but any statement to which they might sign their names would conceal as much as it could possibly dis-

<hr>

[2] In fairness to Professor Horton, it should be noted that he does not always equate consensus with agreement, nor does he believe that complete doctrinal agreement is possible. See the section on "Doctrinal Consensus and Conflict" in *The Nature of the Unity We Seek* (1957), which Professor Horton drafted for the Oberlin Conference.

close. The task before them—and it is greater than the one behind them—is that of defining "presence" and "spirit" in ways which can be understood and accepted by the members of both groups. A willingness to employ the same word or phrase to cover widely divergent views of Christian experience is to be preferred, of course, to merely verbal skirmishing and slogan waving, but it is still very far from having the same thought in mind. Words are the tokens and tools of thought; they may, however, under certain circumstances become the deceptive enemies of thought, and ecumenical theology abounds in instances of this.

Although the search for agreement ought to go on and be encouraged, it still may yield a misleading impression of consensus which we have not actually reached within the ecumenical movement. Do we not learn more sometimes about our common faith through disagreement than through agreement? Certainly, at any rate, our disagreements are more interesting than our agreements; they are likely to reveal more clearly our true principles and loyalties; and they keep us humble before the truth that is in Christ, forbidding us to enjoy a sense of ecumenical achievement which we do not deserve to have.

Have we not perhaps been too quick to agree with each other? In particiular, have not Protestants been too eager to give assent to propositions formulated from within the more catholic traditions regarding Christ, the church, or Christian faith itself? How much has Protestant disillusionment over the piecemeal, splintered character of our religious life had to do with this acceptance? May there not be something just a little compensatory about our preoccupation with the *Una Sancta*? It would be a rare and perhaps rash Protestant theologian who could give a firm, honest No to questions such as these.

Then, too, it must be asked whether the surprising amount of agreement that has been secured already represents a basic unity upon fundamental Christian matters. The slogan "In essentials unity, in nonessentials charity" is undoubtedly a good one; but it seems to suggest to many that what is essential may be defined as that which can be agreed upon, which the nonessential is the realm of stubborn difference. However, this does not at all follow. Only fuzzy and wishful thinking can suppose that, since agreement is itself essential to the ecumenical advance, that on which agreement can be reached is altogether central or at least basic to the understanding of our faith. Charity does not mean tolerance only, but loving acceptance of the other grounded in God's acceptance of us all in Jesus Christ. And unity does not mean agreement only, but belonging to one another because—and not in spite of—the varieties of gifts bestowed upon us by God through our faith in his Son.

Let us then seek wider and deeper agreement within Christendom, but let us not assume that a reunited church is necessarily a unanimous one. It is not so much disagreement as institutional rigidity and isolation that divides our churches from each other at the present time. We often do not know one another well enough to disagree; it would be a sign of more robust health in the church of Christ if we did. Only in a conformist age like ours can agreement have such high priority and disagreement seem a bothersome remainder. Too often, moreover, we confuse the democratic, pragmatic methods of consensus building with Christian faith and life, thus misleading others and perhaps deceiving ourselves. It may be laid down that disagreement, always the lifeblood of theology, is equally the *sine qua non* of true ecumenicity. We should not, therefore, go on regarding our "unresolved differences" as threatening church unity whereas agreement furthers and supports that unity; we should explore our differences not as problems to be solved but rather as opportunities for mutual growth in truth and faith. Very often the so-called "hard core of agreement" turns out on closer inspection to be an extremely soft core indeed. It is the core of disagreement, rather, that theologians who are committed to the ecumenical enterprise must probe and penetrate. It is just possible that on taking a second look we may find less agreement than we had hoped for and more disagreement than we had feared. But it may also be possible that as the ecumenical conversation among theologians deepens, agreement will not seem so important as consensus—the steady growing together of the separated churches not despite but through their legitimate theological differences.

I have said "legitimate theological differences," and this phrase deserves a further, almost marginal word. It is true that many of the things which have historically separated our churches and still separate them today are of little or no theological importance.

They belong rather to the social, economic, or political history of Western culture. So important is this area in an understanding of our present divided state that ecumenical studies pay considerable attention to the "non-theological factors" which enter into the making of every church. There are, however, genuinely theological issues which also divide the churches, often indeed a single church. Certain great options in Chistian theology still persist and find support—Pelagianism versus Augustinianism, for example, or Unitarianism versus Trinitarianism, or sacramentalism versus "spiritualism." It is these legitimate theological differences, when and where they exist, which need to be laid bare and grappled with in the ecumenical context and atmosphere of today. Doctrinal consensus is more significant for the future of the church universal than any series of interdenominational agreements can ever be.

Now let us try to be more constructive in our suggestions for arriving at a true consensus, or meeting of minds, within the Christian church. One of the most hopeful signs of our time in American Protestantism is the resurgence of interest in theological matters on the part of Christian laymen. This interest has by no means reached the proportions of a ground swell as yet, but its magnitude is indicated by the many theological handbooks and wordbooks offered to the churches for individual and group study, the revival of doctrinal and biblical rather than "self-help" preaching, and the growing pattern of lay retreats and conferences across the country. It is now clear that the study of theology has been much too professional and clerical in the recent past, and that there is a hunger for theological affirmation and inquiry among lay people which mightily needs to be fed.

In part this hunger may belong to the general search for security, which acts as a powerful motivator both within and outside the church's life. It is, however, marked by elements of self-criticism and of uneasiness with the present working concordat between faith and culture, which is obviously more conformist than Christian. "Lord, I believe; help my unbelief" is the silent prayer of multitudes within the churches who want to believe but do not know what to believe. We should seize the opportunity provided by this renewed aptitude and hunger for theology by broadening the base of theological discussion, through both formal instruction and informal conversation, at the so-called "grass roots" level of lay participation and responsibility. One does not need to go halfway around the world to become theologically knowledgeable and alert. One must learn to talk theology with his neighbors and fellow members in the church, remembering that the understanding of our faith is everybody's task and privilege.

In this way the search for a consensus may go forward even if it should be no more than an agreement to disagree, complementing the process of "filtering down" theological views and issues by a process of "building up" the church of Christ in the unity of faith. The store of "common grace" which Barth and other European theologians admire in our American church life, its neighborliness and friendliness, may be of real help in attaining this consensus and should quickly be put to theological use.

Another suggestion for reaching a consensus has to do with the way in which we conceive the relation between our diverse traditions and the great tradition of the Christian church as a whole. This has recently been the object of careful study by an ecumenical commission appointed for the purpose, whose recommendations for further study deserve careful thought. But the same question can be seen in a more elementary light. Have you ever seen one of those diagrams depicting the history of the church, used by college instructors in courses explaining the rise of modern denominations? It is usually in the form of a large tree with a heavy trunk, the branches growing out of it labeled "Lutheran," "Reformed," or "Anglican," from which again twigs emerge called "Methodist" or "Church of Scotland," putting forth still smaller twigs like "Missouri Synod" or "Universalist." There, it was thought, was the history of the church. It was a history of proliferation and confusion, of multiplicity stemming out of unity, of complication growing from simplicity. This may not have been an entirely worthless symbol for the growth of Christendom; at least it indicated something like organic wholeness and continuity despite breaks and fresh starts made from time to time.

The interesting and valuable thing, as one tried to tell his students, was to follow the movement backward from the leaf to the little twig to the larger twig to the branch to the trunk and down all the way to the roots of the tree. Thus one could see that wherever he happened to stand on the ecumenical tree there was a way back from his own tradition to the main tradition of the church, whose life and strength were made available through this living connection with the sources of one's faith. No matter how strenuous the protest or how complete the change which launched a new form of Christianity into being, there was still this historic ground of oneness and wholeness.

That is the ecumenical principle with regard to our traditions and the tradition upon which, consciously or unconsciously, willingly or unwillingly, they depend. Our unity is in the first instance continuity. That is not merely wishful thinking glossing over deep-seated differences and critical struggles, but the most solid historical fact. It cannot be gainsaid; it can only be granted.

As this is true historically so it is also true theologically. Wherever there is opposition on one level there is affinity on another. It is not what we are against, but what we are for, that constitutes our distinctive witness and worth. When one begins to view the history of the Christian church in this light one sees hitherto unsuspected signs of a central and on the whole consistent body of theological affirmation enduring throughout many centuries. Gnosticism is as far from Christian truth concerning God and man in the twentieth century as it was in the second, though it be disguised today under such names as Christian Science or Unity; Marcionism is, or ought to be, as indefensible in our time as in the first ages of the church, though espoused by writers of such fame as Arnold Toynbee; and Arianism still raises more questions than it can possibly answer about God in Christ, however confidently it is put forth by the devotees of "liberal religion." There is, indeed, something almost perennial about theological controversy, which suggests in the strongest possible manner that there may also be something equally enduring about theological consensus. In some matters, like the doctrine of Christ and the trinity, the church appears to have reached this consensus early in its development, by about the middle of the fourth century. In others, like the doctrine of man or the church, a long-delayed consensus seems finally to be taking slow and painful shape. But the consensus is there. To recognize that it is there, and that one may share in it, is a salutary and bracing thing.

The ecumenical principle seems obvious enough when simply stated, but it is violated over and over again in Christian thinking and speaking. Here, for instance, is the odd idea that everything which happened in the church between the New Testament and Martin Luther ought to be called Roman Catholic. Figures like Augustine or Francis of Assisi, being generally attractive to Protestants as Bonaventura and Ignatius Loyola are not, must be explained as disguised Protestants or Protestants at heart. The fact is, however, that Roman Catholicism is as much a reaction against early Protestantism, founded in the Counter-Reformation and the Council of Trent, as Protestantism is a reaction against medieval Christian ideas and practices. The doctrine of papal infallibility, which is widely regarded as essential Catholicism, is not yet one hundred years old. In terms of our tree diagram, modern Roman Catholicism is a branch off the main trunk just as Protestantism is, and both find source and sustenance in the same roots, however differently it comes to them. As we have already said and must say again a little farther on, the protestant and catholic approaches in theology are perennial because they are complementary to a fuller understanding of our faith. They have, to be sure, become institutionalized, but they must not be identified with their institutional forms.

There is then a genuine historical consensus in Christian theology, represented best perhaps in the ancient creeds and the modern confessions, but also in what may be called the great tradition underlying all our separated traditions. This is not a least common denominator secured by factoring out our disagreements. Rather, it is an organic, growing unity that is larger than each or all of our perspectives and our positions. We have troubled ourselves over constructing an ecumenical minimum when we should have been discovering the ecumenical maximum that already exists through faith in Jesus Christ. That faith, when theologically grasped and structured, is the main trunk on which every branch of Christendom depends. Or, to change the figure to one used by Douglas Steere, it is with us as with the spokes of a wheel; the nearer we are to the hub, the nearer we come to each other.

IV   One may also look at the search for a consensus in terms of what might be called stages of concern. The first object of attention and discussion, once the ecumenical movement had gotten under way, was quite naturally the Church itself. What are the marks or "notes" of the Church? What makes it what it is?

How shall we conceive the Church in relation to Jesus Christ, the fallen yet redeemable world, the Kingdom of God? What does belonging to it, taking part in its ministry of sacrament and service, have to do with the divine plan of salvation? Answers to these questions constitute, of course, the doctrine of the Church. Asked, however, in the newer ecumenical context they acquire unprecedented urgency and practicality.

One wonders, looking back, whether it might not have proved more fruitful to begin with other matters such as the Lordship of Christ, Virgin Birth, eschatology, or the authority of Scripture. Concentration upon the Church itself laid down the lines of controversy early and perhaps tended to harden them. But they would have been sharp enough regarding these other matters anyway, and at all events we should have had to face the question about the Church sooner or later. Discussion on the Church was very soon polarized about the catholic and protestant conceptions of the ministry, sacraments, and ecclesiastical authority. Only Anglican and Orthodox theologians seemed able to move back and forth between these poles, offering various kinds of ecumenical bridge for our consideration.

Is the Church the extension of the incarnation? Is the service of holy communion the repetition of Calvary? Is the minister (or priest) a delegate or deputy of Christ who exercises his spiritual power by right of apostolic succession? Or is the Church to be understood in terms of believing discipleship rather than of saving Lordship? Shall the meaning of the communion service be confined to that of a memorial inducing confession and repentance through meditation on the example of our Lord? And is the minister set apart by the congregation which he serves, in God's name, to lead his fellow members "in lowly paths of service free"? It soon became plain, as it should have been apparent all along, that there is a world of difference between these two ways of regarding the Church, and yet the story of this stage in searching for a consensus is not wholly one of fixed opposition and contradiction. There have been cracks in the armor of both protestant and catholic defenders, and at least a nascent willingness for each to hear the other out.

Some illustrations of this last remark may be in order. The conception of the communion service as the Eucharist or thanksgiving catches up some valid emphases in both catholic and protestant approaches; the Lutherans have done us much good here, as in Bishop Brilioth's monumental book on *The Eucharistic Sacrifice*, which is both truly comprehensive and consistent theologically. Another telling instance of ecumenical thinking is the sacramental theology of the Benedictine monks of Maria Laach, whose idea of the Mass as "re-presenting" the saving work of Christ rather than as merely repeating it has much to commend it to both poles of the present discussion. True, much more work needs to be done in the definition of "presence" which is implied here, most notably along the lines laid down by the Christian philosophy of Gabriel Marcel. But real theological progress is already being made, as old defensive rigidities are given up for more generous and spacious modes of Christian thought.

Helpful as these detailed studies and contributions are in the long run, the larger question of the nature of the Church remains ecumenically open. Thus far we have not gotten much beyond describing—one could scarcely call it defining—the Church by means of complementary analogies which are forever threatening to become antithetical. There is the Church visible over against the Church invisible—the contrast and yet connection between the church on the corner, so to speak, and "Zion, city of our God." There are the Church militant and the Church triumphant, to both of which some would now add the Church expectant. And there are other similar symbolic contrasts within which our ecumenical thinking must be done.

Among them is one pair of analogies which deserves closer study and discussion by church people everywhere. These are set forth and analyzed with much care in F. W. Dillistone's book, *The Structure of the Divine Society*. He calls them the organic and the covenantal analogies. To think of the Church as an organism in which the whole controls the parts and each part functions uniquely but authentically within the whole is to go back, of course, to the great Pauline figure of the body of Christ. It is certainly the dominant analogy in present-day ecumenical theology. How tremendous a symbol it is, not only for church order and organization but for the Christian life itself! By it the meaning of "membership," for example, is greatly enhanced and deepened, coming to mean in the fullest sense participation or incorporation into the life in Christ (see Theo. Preiss' remarkable book of essays on this latter theme). On such terms as these one really does *belong* to the church. More than that, the various forms of church life-and-work, faith-and-order, have their all-embracing structure and all-empowering source. This is an immensely appealing analogy for the nature of the church, and who will deny that it is also a convincingly true one?

But the covenantal symbol also has much truth in it. Before we can be incorporated into the Church, we must be called into it. Indeed, the Church itself is just such a called-out grouping of men and women, as the Greek word *ecclesia* suggests. It is the people of God, constituted a people not by natural bonds of kinship, nationhood, or race but by God's own call to them. His calling is at the same time his choosing them, his "election" of them. Why God so chooses is a mystery known only to him, "hid in the eternal counsels of God," as the Calvinist phrase puts it. This choice and call has nothing to do with human merit or achievement and so does not make of the Church a spiritual *élite*; but it has much to do with the human response of wondering, obedient faith. All that one can do when God's call comes to him is to hear and make answer with his trusting and loyal life, or else deny God utterly in sinful freedom. The prophets of the Old Testament filled in the details of this great theme, and St. Paul in his letter to the Romans applied it to the meaning of Christian existence in the Church.

Now it is Dillistone's contention, and surely he is right, that neither of these analogies for describing the nature of the Church can stand without the other. What makes the Church an organism is precisely God's call and deed "to us-ward" in Jesus Christ. And yet we know ourselves to be called because we are called together, made one in God's call and choice. Both symbols are in the highest degree ecumenical, as they stress the unity made possible to us in Christ and made actual through our faith in him. They are not simply different ways of saying the same thing theologically, but they need to be held together in the doctrine of the Church.

Taken together, these analogies make plain a truth which has been coming home to us in this first stage of concern—that the question about the Church must be answered in terms of Christ, and the question about Christ must be answered in terms of God. In this sense we have been getting more "orthodox," that is, accepting more and more for our own thinking the substance of the historic Christian consensus on these matters. One would like to claim, and there is reason to support it, that we have actually been growing into theological maturity under the impetus of the ecumenical movement in our day.

Another stage of concern has focused upon the actions and meanings which constitute Christian worship. This in part grew out of the recognition that since "our unhappy divisions" were not primarily theological in nature they might very well be liturgical. But it very soon became obvious that what was required was a theology of liturgy in which these differences might be not only spelled out but also understood in light of ecumenical thinking about the Church. Some, of course, sought to give theological justification for the differences, particularly their own; the greater part of the discussion, however, was given to analysis and understanding of the acts and values characteristic of Christian worship of many kinds.

To this stage belongs, for example, the lively exchange between Barth and Cullmann over baptism in which Barth takes the Baptist position with regard to infant baptism, but on theological rather than scriptural grounds, while Cullmann as a New Testament scholar defends infant baptism as practiced by the majority of the historic churches. The basic issue is between baptism as the rite of initiation into churchly Christian life, made valid by the decision of the one baptized, and baptism as the rite of incorporation into the body of Christ, made valid by God's own grace toward those who may not know they have received it. The interesting thing is to see how each position really implies the existence and worth of the other as well. Thus, if baptism is for those who have already made the decision of faith, it presupposes Christian nurture under the guidance of the churches to which they belong, and this in turn suggests a service of dedication or christening as the young life is lifted up to God in recognition of the responsibility of parents and church for that life. And on the other hand, if baptism is for little children seen as the tokens of God's love utterly unmerited by man, it presupposes no less strongly that the child himself will ratify or confirm this action of the church on his behalf later on in a public and decisive way.

Here is just the sort of issue which particularly commends itself to lay study and discussion in our churches. Another in the same area has to do with the mode or manner of baptism. Baptist preference for total immersion goes back for its validation to Jesus' own baptism at the hands of John, about which we have been learning more from the discovery of the Dead Sea Scrolls. Immersion is even more powerfully justified on symbolic-theological grounds in terms of St. Paul's conception of dying and rising with Christ. Baptism then becomes the threat of death to sin and the renewing of life in faith. Obviously it presupposes an adult recipient. However, the other mode of baptism practiced in our churches, sometimes called "sprinkling" with disdainful inaccuracy, also has biblical and theological rights to exist. It goes back to the ritual of anointing, being marked for the service of God, mentioned many times in the Old Testament. Its meaning can perhaps best be suggested in the words of the Psalmist, "Thou hast laid thine hand upon me."

Hence both meanings and modes of Christian baptism have reality and significance and must be allowed to exist side by side as precious, complementary ways of acting out the truth about God's relationship to man revealed in Jesus Christ. The wholeness of the Church forbids exclusiveness or absolutism in these matters and makes mandatory the most searching, self-critical generosity and "mutual recognition" as together we move ecumenically forward.

Another focus of considerable interest in the field of worship has been that of sacramental theology itself. Essays on the meaning of the Lord's Supper have been numerous, and some have been exceedingly provocative and worth while. Older books, like Bishop Wilhelm Stählin's *The Mystery of God*, continue to exert their benign and stimulating influence, as do more recent volumes such as Dom Gregory Dix's *The Shape of the Liturgy*—two books which every Christian minister should own and ponder. Biblical theology has been of great assistance here, especially in pointing up the relation of sacrament to sacrifice, in assessing the eschatological dimension of the Supper, and in re-evaluating the old controversy between priestly and prophetic elements in Christian worship generally. Along this last line, the claims of the sacrament and the sermon to be the heart or climax of worship have been frankly faced; and it now appears that a full diet of Christian worship should include both, as in the early period of liturgical development when instruction and edification were complemented by celebration and consecration. So we seem to be returning to something like an ecumenical perspective in the matter of worship, and our actual services are already beginning to reflect something of this ampler, truer atmosphere.

Enough has now been said to indicate the new accent in contemporary theology touching Christian worship. It is also, surprisingly, an old accent as well. It conceives theological advance chiefly in terms of revival or renewal, just as it sees church union primarily as a reunion or a reawakening to our oneness and wholeness given in Jesus Christ. Is it not astonishing, but deeply heartening too, to realize that the newest thing in theology is often the oldest? The question of what constitutes theological progress cannot be answered in terms of mere novelty or accumulative increase, for theology is the stewardship of a mystery that is open only to faith —a mystery which deepens the more it is penetrated by the faithful mind of man.

A third stage of concern which has just begun to engage attention deals with the non-theological factors, as they are usually called, determining our present divisions within Christendom. It is both humbling and healthy for us to realize how much the forms of present-day church life owe not to doctrinal but to cultural sources—that is, to such factors as racial inheritance, language structure, nationalism, social change. And it would be quite wrong simply to oppose Christianity and culture on the grounds (criticized in the first two chapters of this book) that a pure Christianity is possible and that human culture as it stands is through and through the product of sin instead of faith. We must recognize not only that we do not have Christianity in a pure state—see Kierkegaard's *Attack Against Christendom*—but also that many aspects of human culture show traces of Christian influence and origin. The whole question of non-theological factors, therefore, is enormously complicated. It belongs to the larger question to which we have paid so much attention in these pages, that of the relationship between faith and culture generally.

No theologian can possibly deal with this question alone. It requires the work of many experts in specialized fields—sociologists, psychologists, economists, political scientists, and others. Studies of population growth and mobility, for example, are indispensable for understanding the form of the church which is developing in present-day America. The pressures of an industrial and technical society need to be charted and comprehended before they can be assessed theologically. Many other illustrations come immediately to mind. The churches have here another opportunity to make fuller use of lay resources and leadership in matters where theologians themselves are laymen (in the secularized sense of that word, which means those uninstructed and inexpert in a given field).

This growing awareness of how non-theological, really, many of the factors are which enter into theological judgment and affirmation is entirely salutary. There is no built-in sanctity, no special privilege, pertaining to theology as such; it is as circumstantial and relative as everything else that human beings do, and should be even more conscious that such is actually the case. This treasure, too, we have in earthen vessels. Theology is not in the business of making claims for itself or for Christianity, but for what God has done in Christ. This need not prevent theologians, however, from seeking to spell out the requirements of a responsible society or from making proximate judgments in those areas where human living and Christian believing must be done.

V   It is time to summarize these reflections on theology as consensus. Let us do so by means of several concluding propositions. The first is this: we have been learning to respect the theological force of the polar principles which have been termed protestant and catholic. It is by now fully clear that the one cannot be reduced to the other any more than it can be absolutely opposed to the other. No consensus can be reached which neglects or overrides the claims of either pole in Christian thinking. The protestant principle that no statement or institution ought to be regarded as divine, that nothing said or done by man is to be held binding upon God, needs always to be kept in balance with the catholic principle that nothing in human existence or in the natural world is so fallen or sin-ridden that it is incapable of reflecting the glory of the Most High. The prophetic warning stands side by side with the sacramental assurance. A Christian theologian who is ecumenically concerned lives somehow at the juncture of these two principles and knows that he must be faithful to them both, emphasizing one as his own situation may require without ever losing sight of the other.

Secondly, a living church must be forever under the judgment of the living God. As always, movement is the sign of life and makes all the difference between a body and a corpse. This means that the churches as we know them and the Church whose life pulses through them—however feebly—are alike to be measured by nothing less than the stature of the fullness of Christ. They are as vessels to treasure, means to end, instrument to purpose, with respect to God's plan for the healing of the nations and the saving of all men. We of the churches are the pilgrim people of God; our life-and-work, faith-and-order are to be prized not for their inherent sanctity but for their serviceableness to God's will. Indeed, it is precisely their serviceableness that gives them whatever sanctity they may claim. This is but to say again that they are broken symbols, participating to be sure in the reality to which they would lead us, but always willing to be broken open and remade that God may be more plainly revealed and thankfully adored. Yes, the Church itself is a broken symbol of God; and the Kingdom of God embraces both Church and world while at the same time surpassing both.

And the third proposition is this: it is the doctrine of the Holy Spirit, more than any other, which helps us best to understand the meaning of church and churchmanship in our own time and place. We are intended by God to become the downward, outward thrust of his Spirit among men, the Spirit which like the wind blows wherever it will, yet which enlivens, encourages, and enlightens our own spirits. To believe in the Holy Spirit means that wherever the Church goes, God has been there before the Church. It means not only that God has given us a world to be redeemed, but that he has bestowed upon us his own power and light for redeeming it. Our task therefore is not to house or manage the Spirit of God but to discover and express it. This makes us all his ministers or priests, sharing alike in the gifts and fruits of the Holy Spirit.

Finally, the wholeness of the Church depends both initially and ultimately upon the wholeness that is to be found in the gospel of Christ. It is not a synthesis or merging of opinions and viewpoints that we seek in trying to voice the common mind of the Christian churches; that might very well be tantamount to saying that what everybody believes nobody believes, which is always the danger in looking for some least common denominator sure to gain general but lukewarm approval. What we are after in our search for theological consensus is the restoration and re-newal of the Church in the midst of the churches. We shall bring to light the unity of faith within the whole Church only as we take the whole Christ for our Lord, the whole gospel for our life, and the whole world for our parish.

Theology as Invitation

O taste and see that the Lord is good!
—Psalm 34:8

I   There is an old and honorable kind of Christian theology known as apologetics. For some time past it has been under a cloud of suspicion as theologians have abandoned earlier efforts to commend Christianity to what was then called the modern mind. It is significant, however, that in our own contemporary situation, which is post-modern in its disillusionment with many of the axioms and assurances shared by thoughtful people over the last three hundred years, apologetics should be coming back. In this final chapter it is my intent to show why, and also to suggest what ought to be the character of Christian apologetics in our immediate theological future.

A good place to begin is with a careful look at the word "apology" itself. Today, in ordinary speech, it seems to carry the meaning of an excuse. I apologize when I have done someone a wrong or hurt in order that I may be restored to friendly relationship with him. My apology is likely to take the form of an explanation which is capable of disarming criticism and forestalling judgment. In explaining my conduct I hope to render it excusable in the eyes of the one who has been offended. There are thus two motives for apologizing: the first, to show the other that I am essentially trustworthy despite what has happened; the second, truly to make amends by throwing myself on the other's mercy;

and there can be no question as to which of these motives ought
to be the stronger. It is always for the sake of being restored to
fellowship that apologies are made, and if this is not the case
they are only alibis.

The old conception of Christian apologetics is both clarified and
obscured by contemporary word usage. Apologetics meant defending the Christian faith against intellectual attack. It was provoked
by misrepresentation and opposition and therefore went hand in
hand with polemics. An astute and knowledgeable theologian did
not apologize for Christianity in our modern sense, nor was he
"apologetic" about the defense he offered. He realized that he
had to attack pagan error and defend Christian truth at one and
the same time. His purpose was to make out a good, substantial
case for his faith in the midst of ideological conflict and spiritual
confusion. He addressed himself to those who did not share the
faith and who, unless he did his work well, were likely to go on
misunderstanding or disdaining it.

At the same time, the Christian apologist was well aware that
something had gone wrong, that understanding between faith and
the world was becoming increasingly difficult, and that it was up
to theologians to remedy and if possible redeem the situation. The
church may not have felt itself to be at fault in producing conflict,
but it did feel itself to be responsible for overcoming it. Not
institutional self-justification but the winning of the world-mind
for the gospel, not propaganda but persuasion, was the apologist's
aim.

There were differences of stance and emphasis, of course. Some
apologetic theologians were "soft" on paganism and used every
opportunity to borrow and adapt non-Christian terms or ideas
for presenting Christian truth. One whole side of Pauline theology,
much neglected of late, reveals this sort of intellectual flexibility
and generosity toward Graeco-Roman ways of thinking, yet without ever forsaking the central Christian affirmations. An even
more liberal attitude toward pagan thought marks the work of
later theologians like Justin Martyr and Clement of Alexandria,
who make Christian use of Stoicism and Platonism for apologetic
purposes. On the other hand, thinkers like Tertullian and Cyprian
take a much firmer line against paganism; their work is still done
in an apologetic situation but they do not want the Christian

faith to be contaminated by pagan influences and they make their case for it primarily by stressing elements of challenge and contradiction. Yet both types of theological response are in the last analysis apologetic in the sense that they are equally aware of the need for defending the truth of faith in the face of indifference and opposition. Part of the greatness of Augustine is that he sums up in himself both kinds of Christian apologetics, knowing when and where to take a strong stand against paganism and how to appropriate its insights to the perspective of his own profound faith in Christ the truth.

It was also Augustine who heralded the changing conception of apologetics which marks the modern period. Two illustrations must suffice. Blaise Pascal, scientist and mystic, conceives his "Apology for the Christian Religion" along the old lines of a tightly reasoned proof capable of securing the conviction of the non-believer, but what he leaves to the world instead is a loosely woven pattern of meditations, arguments *ad hominem,* notebook jottings called the *Pensées.* And in the nineteenth century Cardinal Newman writes his *Apologia* in the same personal vein, describing his own intellectual and spiritual pilgrimage and making of his Christian experience an argument for faith. Both the *Apologia* and the *Pensées* are eminently personal documents of self-disclosure in which the stating of the case for Christianity is cast in the form of the author's own confession and reflection, coming to the reader with the persuasive authority of a mind renewed and a life decisively reoriented.

The feature of apologetic theology, both ancient and modern, which is most noteworthy, however, is that of Christian invitation. This is what gives tone and style to an apology as distinct from a catechism or a system of doctrine. In every instance, the apologist is inviting someone else to share his faith. His invitation may be general or specific, enthusiastic or hesitant, but an invitation it most assuredly is. Theological apologetics has worn many faces and weathered many moods; but whether tough or tender, gracious or peremptory, it has made an overture to the non-believer, put the matter of the Christian faith clearly up to him, and asked for his acceptance of its truth. In one form or another it has been moved by a desire to extend the hospitality of the household of faith to those not yet within its circle.

Apologetics, then, is the theology of invitation, and as such it is but the logical development of the Christian gospel itself. The good news of God, who identifies himself with us and imparts himself to us in Christ, belongs not to Christians but to the world. It is ours not to keep but to give. Moreover, says the apologist, this news is not too good to be true; and he makes it his business to show just how true it is. The gospel not only constitutes and orders his thought but controls his purpose and shapes his task. As God extends his invitation in Christ, so the Christian adds his own. If he does his thinking in the spirit of the gospel, he will soon learn that he too must identify himself with those to whom he would impart the truth of faith. When all is said and done, the apologetic theologian remains a message bearer from God to the world, and his message is in the form of an invitation to faith.

In this light we can begin to understand more clearly and profoundly the renewed apologetic accent in contemporary theology. But there are bound to be objections which must be considered and answered, objections to the very notion of theology as invitation. There is, first, the question of the position in which this view of apologetics places the theologian. Does it not push him so far out toward the circumference of the "theological circle" that perhaps he is no theologian at all? Cannot the process of identifying oneself with unfaith, even for the purpose of overcoming it, become also a deed of theological self-destruction? As one might expect, Karl Barth makes this criticism. In apologetics, he writes, "faith must take unbelief seriously and itself not quite seriously, and therefore secretly or openly ceases to be faith."[1] Since this objection amounts to denying that apologetics is theology, or even a proper task for Christian believers, it should be carefully weighed.

That there are real dangers in the position of the apologist cannot be gainsaid. We have already spoken of the way in which faith itself involves great risks. But this is not to admit that the stance of the apologist is essentially dishonest, devious, or unstable. One may in fact ask whether any sort of Christian theology is possible at all which does not take unfaith seriously, and whether taking unfaith seriously is necessarily marked by a lessening or

[1] Karl Barth, *Doctrine of the Word of God* (Edinburgh, 1936), Vol. I, Part I, p. 30.

weakening of faith. The history of Christian theology bears abundant witness that unless faith has to be defended it will never need to be defined. There is no orthodoxy without heresy or at least the threat of heresy. But heresy comes from within as well as outside the theological circle and represents unfaith at work in the very midst of the community of faith. The theologian must therefore take it very seriously indeed, if only to confront and confound it. The classic creeds of Christendom are not themselves apologetic documents, but they presuppose and reflect the work of thinkers who take unfaith seriously enough to set forth faith in contrast to it.

Is it fair to Clement, Pascal, Cardinal Newman, or C. S. Lewis to assert that taking unfaith seriously means the diminution of one's own faith? The conception of apologetics as a theology of invitation means that the overture to unfaith has its source directly in Christian faith itself. It means that since the gospel is for the world it must be brought to the world, and that when this happens the gospel is not left behind. Thus faith does not fear exposure to unfaith but demands it. The experience of the great Christian apologists certainly seems to indicate that such an exposure may even be necessary for the very growth of one's faith, not merely for its articulation and definition. And it is in terms not merely of a stiffening and hardening of faith as it encounters unfaith but of a generous overture out of the fullness of faith toward unfaith that growth and maturing occur. Barth appears to think of theology as issuing challenges to unfaith to come out and fight but without allowing theologians to take part, as it were, in any hand-to-hand combats or to spy out the terrain and gauge the strength of the enemy. And in any case, this whole notion of unfaith as really anti-faith cannot stand. Without communication there cannot even be confrontation; and without an invitation, issued in good faith, there can be no communication.

The second objection to our view of apologetics as the theology of invitation may be put in the form of a question: How does this differ from evangelism, and does it not confuse theology with preaching? In answer, let us say that while theology is not evangelistic it must always strive to be evangelical, since it derives both source and standard from the Christian gospel. But this answer needs to be spelled out a bit further. The difference between

preaching and theology is like that between cooking and dietetics
—in short, between an act and the theory of that act. Yet the
fact that preaching and theology are functionally distinct does not
mean that they proceed in isolation from each other, or that they
cannot go on concurrently and interdependently. Indeed they are
and should be so related. Since theologians write and teach they
aim to influence and persuade, no less than preachers do. Charles
Duthie of Edinburgh has well and wisely shown in a recent
volume, *God in His World,* that there is a theology or Christian
rationale which underlies every worthy sort of evangelistic effort,
and he rightly sets the whole enterprise of evangelism in the
context of an "engagement with the world."

It also may be said, replying to this criticism, that whereas the
object of preaching or evangelism is to convert, that of apologetic
theology must be to persuade and convince. It is always concerned
with winning a hearing for truth in the mind of another and
therefore must stand squarely against any form of Christian anti-
intellectualism. Yet I have chosen the word "invitation" rather
than "persuasion" to indicate the nature of the apologist's task
because it should be made clear that there is more involved here
than merely "putting across the message" or transferring ideas
from one mind to another. Our present-day view of intellectual
communication has tended to become so mechanical and imper-
sonal that it seems important to insist upon the fully human
context within which alone it can take place. Only as the sharing
of faith occurs at the level of the mind's acceptance of an invitation to truth can there be any possibility of a valid or durable
conversion. It is the business of a Christian apologist to secure
that acceptance by offering that invitation.

There will probably always be some Christian apologists whose
effort takes the form of defending the faith, and others who make
their aim that of inviting non-believers to share it. The two approaches are temperamentally incompatible but not logically antithetical. Most of us find ourselves taking both approaches in the
course of our lifework. My conviction that invitation is the
stronger motive for apologetic endeavor does not imply a lack of
sympathy for a more militant, vigilant dealing with the non-
believer where the occasion demands it, or that in some cases
the most acceptable invitation may not prove to be the most

robust defense. Yet the defense of faith need not be, in the psychological sense, defensive. As Paul Tillich has brilliantly demonstrated, Christian theology can be both systematic and apologetic, which means that all theology partakes of the nature of an invitation rather than a sheer confession; it is a sharing of the truth of faith. Theology as invitation, in short, means speaking the truth in love.

II   This view of theology derives considerable force from the greatly changed situation in which the Christian faith finds itself with respect to human culture at the present time. Not too long ago we were accustomed to draw sharp, clean lines between Christianity and secularism. The premise here was that of conflict; the program for theology was one of heightening the contrast and posing the alternatives. "The church against the world" was a favorite Christian slogan. But today we have a more profound sense of the world's estrangement from the church, and also a more humbling sense of the extent to which the world has entered the church. More important still, we have been rediscovering the world not as a threat to the purity of the church's confession of Christ but as the object of what Charles Forman calls "God's shockingly indiscriminate love." It is after all the world and not solely or chiefly the church which, according to our faith, God gave his Son to save.

In consequence we are no longer so sure of the lines we formerly found it possible to draw. We have been brought up short by the realization that the problems are not all on one side and the solutions all on the other. We have learned that there is an unconscious witness to the gospel which the world can often give more effectively than can the church. Some of our most insidious enemies have turned out to be those of our own household. All this has sobered and in fact shaken many of us who profess and call ourselves Christians. It has overturned distinctions and uprooted definitions. Thus have new occasions been teaching us new duties, in theology as elsewhere.

One of the marks of this change is the recognition that every situation is a missionary situation. We do not need to go halfway around the world to encounter paganism and heathenism; we know them to be in ourselves. Still less can we assume that we are givers while non-Christians are receivers of the gospel, because we have been taught by them much of the meaning of that gospel. Even the difference between foreign and home missions has ceased to be illuminating; in one sense missions are foreign, as they are the Christian response to the fact of an alienated world, yet in another sense all missions are home missions, for they imply and intend the oneness of the world in Christ. These are some of the things that are meant in saying that every human situation is perforce a situation calling for the Christian mission, which, as D. T. Niles remarks, is chiefly "one beggar telling another where to get food."

We are witnessing in our time not so much the confident expansion of Christianity as the intensification of its sense of mission. Since the gospel, in the familiar words of Emil Brunner, is both gift and task, it cannot even be possessed unless it is shared. It is an idle question whether personal commitment or social outreach must come first, as they belong together in the economy of God. In any case, the Christian faith is something which by its very nature must not be kept to itself; it must be given away in order to exist.

Therefore, if anything is clear, it is that the churches need to discover how to escape their confinement in accustomed ruts of organization, speech, and missionary methods. We see now, more plainly than we have for many years past, that in order to be itself the Church must go out of itself into the world for the sake of the world's redemption. Naturally this will involve risk. There is the risk of being misunderstood not only outside but also inside the churches, as we go beyond tolerating opposition and rebellion and begin to welcome it, appreciating its honest and even Christian qualities. There is the risk of being called too experimental and *avant-garde*, too remote from the "grass roots" of common religious life. And there is the risk of having to act and speak with explorative tentativeness instead of self-possessed assurance.

But these risks, as Truman Douglass points out, are inherent in our Christian discipleship in a world where the only safety lies in taking risks. They should be foreseen and calculated, which means having a fundamental, comprehensive understanding of both our situation and our message. At the present juncture this can best be provided by the very conception of theology as invitation which we are describing here. If, as it appears, a new apologetic thrust is in the making, it will require the most astute sort of guidance and direction from the theological task force of the churches.

Many of us have found illuminating and helpful Tillich's idea of the "method of correlation" developed in the first volume of his *Systematic Theology*. Without presuming to give a detailed analysis, we may briefly compare and contrast this method with the approach here set forth. Tillich looks to the arts and the philosophy of our period to discover the questions which our world is asking—questions about the character of reality, about selfhood, about estrangement from and reunion with other persons, about many aspects of our "ultimate concern." The theologian, he says, is one who must listen carefully to these questions, without distorting or rephrasing them to suit his convenience, hearing them just as they come to him from the world in which he lives and does his work.

But having heard the questions, the theologian must give answers to them; hence Tillich's conception of an answering theology which adjusts the Christian message to the situation by fitting its answer, so to speak, into the vacuum of the question asked. Before this can happen, however, the theologian must show that he understands the question and is not simply using it for purposes of his own, that he has made it his question too, so that the answer, when it comes, will genuinely resolve the difficulty which has been expressed. Theologians, then, must be thoroughly and personally acquainted with at least some of the areas of culture in which such questions are emerging, though of course no theologian can be well acquainted with all.

With everything that Tillich says concerning the importance of a theological grasp of artistic, psychological, or philosophical materials one must, I think, be in complete accord. The first two chapters of our book presuppose and underscore this agreement. But Tillich's whole scheme of situation and message, question and answer raises some vexing issues for the theologian, who in a sense is caught between them. In this book we have not been as confident as Tillich is that culture always asks the questions while theology gives the answers. Very often a theologian has to ask questions of the questions which are presented to him, or to see questions behind these questions. Furthermore, he must sometimes be made to see that what he offers as an answer may have questionable features which cause him to reconsider and restate his own previous formulation. Some theologians persist in giving answers to questions which are never actually asked, and Tillich's method of correlation can be very useful in preventing this. But does it help the theologian who goes on thinking of his enterprise as basically the furnishing of answers when in fact it may well be chiefly the raising of questions about the answering enterprise itself?

This whole question-answer scheme, in short, is not as simple as it looks and needs a great deal of rethinking. It would be totally unfair to give the impression that Professor Tillich does not realize this; but neither does his correlation scheme provide the structure for it. Much of his thought, in fact, seems to demand another sort of structure, notably his stress in recent writing and lecturing upon the risk and doubt inherent in Christian faith itself. Can I really understand my faith as a body of answers to the questions asked by the world without ceasing to be faithful in the sense of having utter trust in God? Is not my experience of God in the Christian faith one in which questions are put radically to me rather than one in which answers are furnished me for the needy perplexities of others? Moreover, if by Christian vocation and intellectual training I happen to be a theologian, is not my task very largely that of listening to and reflecting upon the world's answers, its own expressions in cultural form of its ultimate concern, rather than transforming them into questions answerable by theology? One can scarcely put the conversation which must go on between theology and culture in the form of a catechism, without doing incredible violence to the nature of that conversation itself.

Therefore it seems preferable to think of theology as invitation instead of correlation, granted that some correlative effort is always required. An answering theology is in the first instance a listening theology, and finally an inviting theology; this is what gives its answers such relevance and fruitfulness as they may have. If theology is not to be conceived in terms of a rejoinder or rebuttal on the one hand, or as a fitting of doctrinal keys into various cultural locks on the other, the correlation scheme must be—as the current barbarism has it—"de-emphasized." What has to be questioned most of all is just this idea of message and situation in a kind of parallel confrontation with each other, and it must be questioned on decidedly Christian, theological grounds.

Two brief remarks may be made touching the latter point. One is that we do not have the Christian message in self-contained dogmatic form, nor do we exist in situations totally devoid of Christian meaning and worth. The gospel does not merely "apply" to the world but is among other things an interpretation of that world. Hence a Christian is bound to read the situation differently, and it may well not be the same situation as it would be without this faith-interpretation. The concept, or rather metaphor, of the "application" of Christianity is, I believe, both unfortunate and sterile. Its message is not added to or laid upon the human situation in the simple fashion which this way of speaking suggests. Much apologetic theology consists in discovering within a situation its Christian significance, if only in some preparatory or potential sense; the classic example here is of course Paul's address to the "very religious" Athenians who worshiped an unknown God.

The second remark is that the systematic and apologetic aims in theology are not contradictory but complementary and even interdependent. No one in our time has been more helpful in making this clear than Tillich himself, but his method of correlation does not give adequate expression to this insight. Instead of trying to have it both ways, as Tillich does, why should we not grant that the two aims throw light upon and fortify each other? Whatever comprehensiveness and consistency Christian theology may claim for itself is, if not a result, at least a function of its engagement with the world. And such an engagement, as we have already made clear, is directly required and demanded by the character of Christian faith as it attempts to understand itself.

A bit earlier we ventured a description of theology as invitation in biblical terms as speaking the truth in love. We may now add a second biblical word: such theology is giving to everyone who asks a reason for the faith that is in us. What this means is not that a theologian must wait to speak until he has been spoken to, but that he is most at home, even inside the community of faith, with those who seek and ask after God. He uses the tools of reason and moves consciously and purposefully within the milieu of rational inquiry in the sharing of his faith. For this is his reasonable service to God and his fellow men.

III　　Bearing in mind this general perspective of apologetic theology, we shall now focus our attention upon a single instance of it. We shall be considering what is usually called the problem of the relation between Christianity and the other religions. So much has been said and written on this problem, especially in the last few decades, that we cannot hope to do more than sketch the merest outline of a point of view. There are times, however, when it is better to be frankly suggestive than altogether silent, and there can be no doubt that ours is such a period. Arnold Toynbee has predicted that in the next generation, because of the rapid interpenetration of cultures and religions, an individual human being may be able to choose his own faith to a degree undreamt of in the past and present. Already we have many indications of the validity of this prediction—the increasing influence of Zen Buddhism in some circles, the cooperation of Christians with Moslems in joint business enterprises, the religiously polyglot character of many university campuses, the temporary foreign residence of many American families, particularly in Asian countries, and so forth. The problem of Christianity and the other religions is no longer merely a theme for classroom debate or academic conferences; it has already become a thoroughly "existential" one.

We shall be able to indicate only a few of the facets of the problem, and only as they bear upon the new apologetic accent in theology. The first point to be noted is that the sheer fact of religion in the world is a Christian fact. The universality of religion throughout different periods and cultures—its unimaginable complexity but also its astonishing identity—is something which Christians have to understand. It is not merely a datum for the anthropologist or the psychologist, though it is also that. The universal fact of religion should be part of the subject matter of Christian theology itself—perhaps not its central or basic part, but a fact to which all theology must pay attention before its work is done. Can this tremendous fact be comprehended and set forth in Christian terms? What does it mean to the Christian faith that there are other faiths besides Christianity?

Notice that this way of asking the question differs markedly from that in which it is most often put. Ordinarily we tend to pose the question about Christianity and other religions in such a way that it answers itself, or at any rate implies that a satisfying answer can be given. We ask how Christianity can be true in the midst of so many other claims to truth, and then our answer is likely to take the form of what is known as syncretism. There is some truth in all religions, according to this position, even though no one religion can claim to have a monopoly on all truth. This fits in well with the virtue of tolerance so greatly prized in a pluralistic society such as ours, and appears to do rational justice to the undoubted relativity of man's religious experience. Or else we ask how other religions can possibly be true if Christianity is true, and then our answer usually takes the form of what is called exclusivism. The difference between Christianity and the other religions is simply that between truth and error, or at least between knowledge and ignorance of the one true God. This view leaves Christian conviction basically unshaken, provides what is sometimes termed a "motive for missions," and reassures the churches in their work and life at home.

However, neither syncretism nor exclusivism can serve the purposes of Christian theology, as neither really grapples with the issues raised. Each view can be shown to have some theological merit, to be sure. Christianity must sooner or later come to the realization of its own implication in the relativities of culture, understanding that it is in the world as one religion among others. But it must also realize *why* it is in the world, what the grounds of its uniqueness and specific genius are, and how within human culture it may point men to the God who is above culture. Neither exclusivism nor syncretism can possibly do theological justice to the universality of religion and the uniqueness of Christianity at the same time or on the same basis. Each may be used theologically to correct the shortcomings of the other, but both are equally lacking—they may even prove pernicious—where the Christian understanding of the fact of human religiousness is concerned.

Can we reach such an understanding? That is, can we see the universality of religion in terms of the uniqueness of the Christian faith? Is it possible to make sense of the fact of religion in the light of God's purpose for mankind, and not simply as a challenge to our strategy in missionary endeavor or as a standing contradic-

tion to our highly prized truth? I believe we can so understand
it and interpret it, because we must. Both our situation and our
message demand it. On the one hand, we must certainly follow
men like Hendrik Kraemer in holding that there is religion, human
religious experience, over against revelation, the self-disclosure of
God. But this is surely not identical with a distinction between
non-Christian and Christian forms of faith in God—as Kraemer
of course has to allow—for in one sense the Christian religion is
over here on the side of human cultural experience against God's
revelation, and in another sense revelation is to be found invariably
in religious form, since all religion has to do with some divine
revealing act. And on the other hand, we must follow men like
Toynbee or Hocking in saying that revelation, as we know or have
to do with it, appears as a kind of dimension or power of religion
even when it comes as a "bolt from the blue"; it is, in short, our
way of attributing our experience of God to God himself. But
this does not for a moment imply that religion and revelation are
essentially the same, which is the impression one often gets in
reading Hocking and Toynbee. Must we not attempt to make
within experience and for the sake of understanding it a real
distinction between its human shape and its divine source? Does
not our very understanding of religion, all religion, imply at least
the hypothesis of revelation?

We may find needed light on these questions, I believe, in the
thought of Herbert Farmer of Cambridge University, especially
as contained in his Gifford Lectures titled *Revelation and Religion*.
He shows that religion cannot be separated from revelation in any
way that is historically or institutionally advantageous to the
Christian faith precisely because the Christian and biblical understanding of faith prohibits such a separation. Yet he insists that
"there is given to us through the Christian revelation the norma-
tive concept of religion."[2] This is but another way of saying that
religion itself is a Christian fact, which means that it must and
can be interpreted in Christian terms. The way Professor Farmer
works out his position, guarding it against misunderstanding from
both the extremes he wishes to avoid, is well worth following.
It affords precisely the sort of platform on which a theology of

[2] H. H. Farmer, *Revelation and Religion* (New York: Harper, 1954), p.
35; see also chap. III.

invitation can be properly and positively launched, without either surrendering or shrinking the truth of our faith.

In order to deal intelligibly with this problem theologians have habitually made use of a distinction between general and special revelation, or between natural and revealed religion. The second point in our discussion of Christian and non-Christian religion has to do with the propriety and force of this distinction. It is undoubtedly very difficult for me to explain to myself as a Christian the fact that God has evidently appointed other means to fellowship with him than the one which I know uniquely in Jesus Christ. Almost inevitably I begin to think along the lines made possible by this distinction. Why should I not adopt this way of putting a matter which so perplexes me? Why not then say that God has ordained a twofold kind of revealing relationship to men? There is, let us assume, a relationship of God to men which is general and universal, established through nature and culture and explaining the existence of religion; and there is another sort of relationship of God to men which is special and unique, given concretely to those who make their own decisive, obedient response to Christ as the Son of God and explaining the existence of Christianity. Thus I may see God appearing on two levels at once, as it were—on a ground floor which includes all mankind and on a much smaller top floor restricted to Christians, with some sort of stairway leading from one level to the other.

However, in adopting this two-story setback structure for my thought I only compartmentalize religious universality and Christian uniqueness; I do not relate them positively to each other. The question with which I began is still there and in some respects it is sharper, more disturbing than before. And so my thought tends to move on toward the view that special revelation is a particular case or instance of general revelation. Every man's faith looks unique to him, but perhaps it is not as special as it seems. Why not be objective and self-critical and admit that Christianity is but one of the ways in which we apprehend the self-disclosure of God to men? Soon my thought reaches the point along this route where all religions are equally though differently true; each is unique as a particular example of the universal religious dimension of human life, perhaps even of the "collective unconscious" of mankind. The controlling metaphor changes to that of the same mountain with various roads leading to the summit—a favorite image of many college students as they first become aware of this problem.

But my thought cannot rest even here. If all the roads go up the mountain of religious truth and succeed in reaching the top they might be equally true; but the trouble with a conception of this sort in which all religions are equally true is that they are also equally false. There is no way of deciding what is true in a religion except in terms of a least common denominator which any really religious person would be bound to reject. If truth is merely a matter of majority participation or shared equality, then it is certainly not what we mean by truth outside the sphere of religion and its tests are not those we apply to distinguish truth from error. How can I possibly know that all religions are equally true, that any special revelation of God is but a fair sample of general revelation, unless I stand at the top of the mountain looking down at all the roads as they wind up its sides? In short, I would have to be God to know this. I may, for the sake of peace and quiet in this troubled atmosphere, adopt a live-and-let-live equalitarian psychology, but my permissiveness settles nothing regarding truth and actually becomes a way of avoiding grappling with it.

Just here the contribution of Zen Buddhism appears highly significant to many intelligent students of religion today, because it does not abandon the search for religious truth. Instead, Zen identifies that truth with what is the common essence of all religions, although this must be stated negatively and indirectly, since to reduce it to propositions would at once make it untrue. By its most persuasive interpreters, such as D. T. Suzuki and Alan Watts, Zen is presented as at once a judgment upon all religion and the essential truth in every religion. Thus it is called "the religion of no-religion." There is a remark quoted from a Zen master which may help to make this viewpoint somewhat clearer. "When I knew nothing of Zen," said the master, "the mountains were to me merely mountains, and the waters merely waters; when I knew a little of Zen, the mountains were no longer mountains, nor the waters waters; when I understood Zen well, the mountains were again mountains, and the waters waters." So, according to the adherents of Zen, there is a progression of religious insight from habitual acceptance through discriminating detachment back to knowing re-acceptance. What is made possible is a religious transvaluation of religion. In the light of this claim, it is interesting to see how within Zen a particular vocabulary, not to say an *ethos*, develops, how certain texts and maxims become central, lines of influence and dependence are established, and a kind of religiousness, if not a full-fledged religion, takes shape. Yet the accent is always upon a mode of insight rather than upon ideas or institutions, to such an extent that the element of devotion or self-commitment becomes very attenuated if not entirely absent. Realizing this, Zen has been called half-humorously "the no-religion of religion."

There is, when all is said, only one tenable position on the matter of general and special revelation. I cannot regard Christianity, any more than a Moslem can regard Islam, as a particular case of some abstractly universal connection between God and man which can be otherwise known and validated. This means that the only way I can get to general revelation is from special revelation, not the reverse. The only way in which I am able to speak or think of a universal self-disclosure of God to men is from my frankly Christian point of view. Both logically and theologically, I can find no way from the general to the special revelation which does not dissolve the latter. Precisely because I believe God to be who he is through the Word which he has spoken to us in Jesus Christ our Lord, I have the very strong suspicion that his revelation is not confined to me and my fellow believers. It is exactly by reason of God's unique disclosure of himself, his will and way for us and for the world, that I cannot limit God's revelation to Christianity. Because I am related to God through faith in Christ I see more than an ancient covenant re-established, more than a community newly founded. I see a plan of salvation for all mankind laid bare and made effective. And so I must consider and be guided by the universal meaning of this unique revelation. It is the God and Father of our Lord Jesus Christ, not some other god supposedly behind or above him, who is by the same token the God and Father of all men whoever or wherever they may be in his vast domain.

I do not have to turn to Zen Buddhism to learn about the God above all gods, for my own faith has a great deal to teach

me on this score. Nor do I need to go with Karl Barth in declaring
that God reveals himself only through Jesus Christ, if this means
only to believers in Christ, since my own Bible and my own
Church instruct me differently. The more carefully I think about
it, the more I come to understand the special Christian revelation
as the culmination of the universal human revelation, which I
identify with a certain readiness, preparation, or, in Brunner's
word, "addressability" in the hearts of men.

Uniqueness is not necessarily exclusiveness. The "scandal of
particularity" about which so much has been written of late is at
the same time the scandal of universality, as Paul in Romans
sought so strenuously to make plain. "God so loved the world"—
not the Church, or Christianity, but the world—"that he gave his
only-begotten Son": this is a motive for missions which has nothing to do with imposition and indoctrination, with putting
"Mother Hubbards" on Hawaiian natives and the like, but everything to do with invitation and the generous, humble sharing of
our faith. We Christian believe, and believe profoundly, that there
is that in God which is not uttered by his Word but is sent
abroad by his Spirit, and perhaps paradoxically, it is by his Word
that we believe this. That is one important thing meant by
holding that special revelation makes room for, and indeed requires, a conception of general revelation.

A third point to consider as we face the large and intricate
problem of Christianity among the religions is this: we simply
do not find the Christian faith and the revelation upon which it
depends in a pure state. If we did, admittedly the problem would
be greatly changed, but we do not. What we do have is revelation
that is always relative to human capacities and historic conditions,
or else it would not be revelation. There is no way out of these
relativities. Harnack for his generation and Bultmann for our
own have tried brilliantly to extricate us, but despite these and
other efforts Christianity in its pure state cannot be isolated and
controlled; we do not have with respect to it a "laboratory situation" even for the purpose of a theoretical analysis of its essential
meaning. To be a historical faith in a historical revelation is to
be enmeshed inextricably in sinful circumstances and partial perspectives.

True, we can and must seek to identify the gospel, and every failure in obedience or trust is at the same time an approximation to them. Nevertheless the good news of one who was both God and man "crossed for the sins of the world," in Joseph Hardy Neesima's phrase, the revelation of God in Christ by which we judge others and find them wanting in faith, also judges us and finds us wanting. The scandal of particularity cuts both ways. We must never suppose that it is only an offense to the non-Christian; it is a stumbling block to the Christian as well. The scandal of the cross, the stubborn particularity of the claim Christians make for Christ, is in a real sense more offensive and incredible to the believer than to the non-believer, if only because it ricochets back upon the believer in so many unexpected and uncomfortable ways.

Some words of Ralph Waldo Emerson suggest themselves at this point. "First the spirit builds its house," he wrote, "and then the house confines the spirit." There is the history of religion in a nutshell. One sees the truth of Emerson's remark every time a young couple makes a down payment on a house and moves in; soon afterwards, especially in a time of 6 per cent mortgages, the house has begun to clamp down on the spirit which possessed it. A similar process takes place in the larger affairs of mankind and more particularly in religion. What ought ideally to be a liberating and releasing development becomes instead a warping and confining one. We simply do not have the Christian faith, much less the revelation to which it is the response, in a pure state; in consequence the principle by which we judge other faiths is identical with that which judges our own.

The fourth point in what might be termed this theological sketch of world religions is that in every religion God is prior to itself. For a long time now the very word "religion" has been suspect, if not taboo, in Christian theology—at least as a designation for anything that could properly and strictly be called Christian. But the word is clearly indispensable to apologetic and missionary theology and therefore it is quickly being reinstated. In the event that its meaning may have been forgotten, let us recall that it signifies a tying-back or binding-back to God. Religion logically as well as experientially presupposes God. Now this may indeed be, as Farmer says, a colossal assumption to make, but nothing can be plainer than that all religion makes it, however the priority or initiative of God is described. Religiously conceived, human life *means* God or it means nothing. The search for God itself presupposes the God who is sought, even if that search is rebuked or ends in failure, to the mind of the seeker. All the beliefs and practices of religious people in whatever place or period make this colossal assumption and proceed upon it.

To be sure, in saying this we have not proved the existence of God merely by pointing to activities such as prayer and worship; our purpose here is rather to describe human religiousness in terms which religious people themselves would recognize as accurate. Some of us, fortunately I think, did not hear of the priority of God from Barth or Brunner first; we learned it from our Bibles, from Paul and Augustine, from P. T. Forsyth and William Temple and Baron von Hügel, or perchance from Christian poets like Hopkins and Patmore, Herbert and Vaughan. We were taught there that in our faith the priority of God means the initiative of holy love, a love that knows no boundaries and makes no exceptions. We know through Christ that God is love and that he does not reserve that love to Christians, but wills to share it with every one of his creatures. We owe this sovereign, saving love to God himself, and even more do we owe to him our very human capacity for receiving such love and imparting it to others in our turn. Thus in the experience and thought of Christians the divine priority does not mean merely the divine causality but rather the divine generosity, as Gabriel Marcel rightly suggests. It means the initiative of a seeking, gathering, forgiving love coming to us from the very heart of being. Such love by its own nature cannot be kept to itself but must be shared, since sharing is exactly what it is, if that word is taken in an ultimate as well as an intimate sense.

We must be content with pointing out only a few of the implications of this important truth. A theology of invitation does not begin by saying to the unbeliever or non-believer, "See how poor and weak you are! But Christianity has untold spiritual riches and power. Accept Christ, come over to where we are, and you shall have them." Instead, a theology of invitation spreads its feast of Christian truth in the midst of the world, in the midst of its strivings and seekings after God, and in the light of this abundant generosity of God men's need and lack begin to appear. Somewhere Hendrik Kraemer has rightly said that it is not the consciousness of sin that brings men to Christ but contact with Christ that brings men to the consciousness of sin. Is it not always true that only in the presence of perfection does imperfection become known? God's fullness is what reveals our emptiness. His goodness discloses our evil. His will to fellowship shows us our estrangement from him. I would not know my need unless I also knew, however dimly or brokenly, that which alone could satisfy it. It is this prior awareness, or awareness of priority, which leaves me "without excuse," as Paul wrote to the Romans. It is forgiveness, not simply judgment, which heaps "coals of fire" upon my head. It is love that begets love, faith that elicits faith, and hope that inspires hope.

Does not all this put quite a different face upon the missionary motive and message of the Christian faith? It is precisely the so-called exclusiveness of Christianity, its scandal of particularity, that constitutes the ground of its amazing and even shocking inclusiveness. One may readily sympathize with the graciousness and patience which lead some Christians to say that they will make no claims for loyalty to Christ which give annoyance or offense to adherents of other faiths; but the question of truth will not be silenced, and it cannot be settled or even posed by any equalitarian or "comparative" devices, by what is essentially a kind of politics or a kind of etiquette. What we Christians see in Christ is nothing less than the cruciform nature of all human existence itself, taking the cross in the sense of both suffering and victory.

There is a passage in the Apology of Justin Martyr, called by some historians the earliest example of Christian symbolism, which makes this point wondrously clear. "Think for a moment," says Justin Martyr to his pagan reader, "and ask yourself if the business of the world could be carried on without the figure of the cross. The sea cannot be crossed unless the sign of victory—the mast— remains unharmed. Without it there is no ploughing; neither diggers nor mechanics can do their work without tools of this shape. The human figure is distinguished from that of brute beasts solely by having an upright posture and the ability to extend the arms; and also by the nose through which the creature gets his breath, which is set at right angles to the brow, and displays just the shape of the cross."[3] (One thinks here of Rouault's "Holy

[3] In *The Early Christian Fathers* (New York: Oxford, 1956), pp. 83–84.

Face.") And Justin Martyr went on to say that the cross which was carried before the Roman legions into battle as their standard and which was shaped into the mast and the plow was in reality the cross of the suffering, victorious Son of God. The form was already there, and he took it and filled it with Christian meaning. Thinking as a Christian and from within the perspective of his faith, he went forth into the world of strange and alien religions discovering mysterious confirmations and tokens of his own faith.

One may indeed smile today at the extent to which Justin Martyr carried his theology of invitation, the way in which he made the cross say far more than it actually meant to the Romans, who used it without knowing its Christian significance. But surely Justin's instinct was sound and his principle was right. Invitation must first of all mean identification. Quite possibly there will always be something just a little forward and uncalled-for in an act whereby the Christian wills to share his faith with one who is not of his own fold. This is because theological invitation rests so firmly upon the employment of Christian imagination—seeing the other as he must look to God, as one for whom Christ died, as the neighbor whom in Christ's name I am to love.

When we go forth into the world with the message of redeeming and renewing love, we not only carry with us a new symbol or image for the meaning of human existence. We read the old symbols in a new and saving light. We are able to see even more in the non-Christian's situation—not less, but more—than he sees in it himself. And so we speak to men of a God who, just because he is yet unknown to them, or perhaps long forgotten, is still accessible in grace and majesty to them. Theology as invitation seeks not substitution but fulfillment, in relating Christian to non-Christian forms of faith in God.

IV   In conclusion, how may these reflections serve to illumine the task and scope of contemporary theology? In the pages that remain we shall attempt an answer to this question. Earlier in the chapter it was pointed out that apologetics, in the sense of invitation stressed here, is not merely a branch of theology but an inherent feature of all theological work. The truth of Christian faith, which is the proper concern of all theology, does not consist in propositions about God and man, Christ and the Church, eternity and history, although these terms are the poles between which theological reflection always moves. Christian truth is personal truth, engaging the thinker as well as his thought. At its very heart is God's own invitation to be reconciled in believing trust to him. Since theology itself is a response to God's gracious overture in Christ, the love of God with all one's mind, its formulations of Christian truth should be consistent and continuous with that response.

Another relevant consideration is this: The truth of Christian faith is not something which can be possessed first and shared afterwards; we do not think first dogmatically and then apologetically, but the systematic character of theology only begins to appear when communication with non-believers takes place. Apologetics is emphatically not the packaging of Christian truth in attractive shapes and convenient sizes for the multitudes. It ought not to be confused, as many popular books today confuse it, with a kind of promotion or special pleading. What is here at fault is not so much the cheapening of faith itself, although that is grave enough, as the false assumption that Christians have something of their own to give away. That assumption has no place within the Christian mission to the world, precisely because it has no place within the Christian message for the world.

What, in Christian terms, is the meaning of "the world"? Theology has hesitated between two interpretations. There is the interpretation in much of the Fourth Gospel which regards "world" as "the opposition." It is a blanket term for whatever is alien and therefore inimical to faith in Jesus Christ. The world threatens the purity of faith and must be kept at arm's and mind's length. Over and over again in the history of Christian thinking this same view has prevailed, especially in monasticism and pietism. This makes the Christian a kind of counter-revolutionary or at least a fifth columnist, conscious of hostility and alert to the dangers of entanglement; in Nietzsche's phrase, he is a No-sayer to the vitalities and affirmations of worldly culture.

But there is also a second interpretation, and the Gospel of John discloses it quite as much as the first. "World" is that which God loves as his own creation; it is not only the spot on which God puts the man of faith but also the place given him by God for doing the truth and being grasped by eternal life. It is unthinkable, is it not, that what is the object of God's love should be the target of man's fear; is not the world instead the very field so constantly spoken of in the New Testament, in which the seed of the gospel is to be sown and for which it is intended? The Christian therefore must say Yes to the world, not in the sense of approving whatever happens in it but in the sense that he ceases to be threatened by it and courageously involves himself in it. If God so loved the world, can Christian man do less? What then is theology but probing the meaning of life-in-the-world by the standard of God's word and deed in Jesus Christ? What is it, really, but spreading a feast of love-in-truth to which all mankind is invited and therefore welcome and expected? All too often these two aspects of theology, the critical and the invitational, have been set against each other when as a matter of Christian truth they belong together. Such a separation is impossible if the unity of message and mission is to be maintained and declared. What is required, rather, is the fusion within the theologian's perspective of the utmost compassion with intellectual expertness and acuity.

The Christian thinker is not one whose thought is ideologically pure, untainted by the presuppositions and implicit loyalties of the culture which nourishes him. He must be both in the world and not of the world. That means the recognition and acceptance of one's animal ancestry and social responsibility and cultural involvement as part of God's will for one's life and work. It means that one knows himself to be encompassed and enmeshed within the successiveness of history and the spaciousness of nature, without possibility of extricating or withdrawing himself. It means rejoicing with those who rejoice and weeping with those who weep, whoever or wherever they may be. It does not mean taking up a position either of denial or of defiance toward the world.

And it cannot mean this, because the understanding of the truth of faith demands a certain distance from the faith itself. The point must be stated very carefully since it is far from obvious today. Much has been said and written about the impossibility of being objective where one's faith is concerned; commitment and "passionate subjectivity" have been justified and praised. As a reaction against rationalism, cynicism, or indifference such an emphasis has its undoubted place, but one suspects the time for this particular reaction has already passed, in contemporary theology at least. Really to understand one's faith means to look at it afresh, perhaps almost as if it were not one's own, at any rate not as something to be taken utterly for granted. Theologians are often suspected by their fellow Christians of lukewarmness and aloofness toward the ongoing activities of the churches. On the outside, however, theologians are frequently regarded as constituting a kind of propaganda ministry on behalf of actual Christianity. The truth is probably somewhere between these two extremes. A theologian has to be "semi-detached" if he is to grasp the meaning of Christian faith without partisanship or distortion; he can render no real service as theologian to his church if he does not maintain the sort of personal distance that makes genuine understanding possible. But this distance is not identical with mere inquisitiveness or condescension; instead, it is the purposeful putting of oneself in the place of another, the standing back to see better and farther, the employment of reason in the service of true faith. Objectivity and commitment in theology are not static components between which an absolute distinction and decision can be made. They are rather stresses within what Tillich calls the "dynamics" of faith, and are to be used in living equilibrium with each other under the leading of God's Holy Spirit.

That which is a matter of search cannot be simply a matter of course. The truth of faith is not a proprietary or a privileged truth. There is that in it which rebukes and reshapes our preconceptions. Are not God's ways with men likely to be even more strange to those who believe in him through Christ than they are to those who ignore or deny Christ? We are greatly in error if we think that faith is a problem-solving technique or a body of answers in the back of the book. There are reasons coming from the Christian message itself which should prevent our thinking this. When we hear the words of Jesus, "Other sheep have I which are not of this fold," must we not begin to wonder if we really do belong to him? The presence of religion in the world as a fact of human culture stands in judgment upon Christian pretension and exclusivism. Religion, wherever and however it occurs, represents man's capacity for faith in God as well as God's unwearying search for man's eternal good. Since religion, understood in Christian terms, constitutes both an opportunity and a rebuke to Christianity, and since our faith forbids religious segregation and discrimination, every situation in which a theologian stands is necessarily a missionary and apologetic situation. Most of all a

theologian, in the words of Augustine, is "a question to himself";
his faith is not a foregone conclusion but a point of departure
into the truth.

Theology, as Brunner writes, is believing thinking. One does
not take leave of faith when he begins to think about faith, nor
does he abandon the standards and methods of rational intelligence just because he is wholeheartedly a believer. A theologian
believes in order to think, and he also thinks in order to believe.
His belief serves as the springboard of his thought; his thought
becomes the expression of his belief. And both are nourished and
shaped by that engagement with the world to which God calls
us in love and in truth.

To speak the truth in love, then, is always the theologian's task.
This does not mean "getting the message across" by breaking
through the reserve of someone else. It does mean making oneself
vulnerable to the need, concern, and worth of the other. Furthermore it means inviting the other to share what one has found
good, right, and true, because of the command and companion-
ship we have in Christ. The matter has been stringently and
forcefully put by Daniel D. Williams, who writes: "We never
exhaust the meaning of Jesus Christ. All human knowledge is
relevant to our knowledge of him. He does not destroy but
fulfills all other truth, else he would not be the Christ." And it
may be added that we would not be Christians if we did not believe this and live according to it. By the same token, we could
not be Christian theologians if this truth were not central to our
thought.

The first miracle wrought by Jesus at Cana in Galilee has a
meaning for us here. Christian faith itself, when rightly experienced
and understood, is a miracle not unlike that of the water made
wine. When we as Christians read non-Christian literature or
encounter forms of religious faith alien to our own, the water in
them becomes wine. There is often a shock of recognition which
rests back upon the deed of imaginative identification that is
Christian love at its profoundest level. This can only issue in the
very sort of invitation we have been describing—an invitation given
in the spirit of the God and Father of our Lord Jesus Christ, who
bids us to communion with himself and all our fellow men in his
everlasting Kingdom.

Suggestions for Further Reading

Chapter 1

> *The Christian Scholar*, December, 1957—an issue devoted to Christianity and the arts.
>
> *Spiritual Problems in Contemporary Literature*, ed. by Stanley R. Hopper (New York: Harper Torchbooks, 1957).
>
> Paul Tillich, *Dynamics of Faith* (New York: Harper, 1957), chap. III.

Chapter 2

> Karl Heim, *The Transformation of the Scientific World View* (New York: Harper, 1953).
>
> Langdon Gilkey, *Maker of Heaven and Earth* (New York: Doubleday, 1959).
>
> *New Essays in Philosophical Theology* (New York: Macmillan, 1955).
>
> David E. Roberts. *Existentialism and Religious Belief* (New York: Oxford University Press, 1957).

Chapter 3

> Raymond Abba, *The Nature and Authority of the Bible* (Philadelphia: Muhlenberg Press, 1959).

Karl Barth, *Dogmatics in Outline* (New York: Philosophical Library, 1949).

Rudolf Bultmann, *Essays* (New York: Macmillan, 1955).

Paul Tillich, *Biblical Religion and the Search for Ultimate Reality* (University of Chicago Press, 1955).

Chapter 4

J. Robert Nelson, *One Lord, One Church* (New York: Association Press, 1958).

A. C. Outler, *Christian Tradition and the Unity We Seek* (New York: Oxford University Press, 1958).

T. F. Torrance, *Conflict and Agreement in the Church* (London: Lutterworth, 1959).

Chapter 5

H. H. Farmer, *Revelation and Religion* (New York: Harper, 1954).

Hendrik Kraemer, *Religion and the Christian Faith* (Philadelphia: Westminster Press, 1956).

Alan Richardson, *Christian Apologetics* (New York: Harper, 1947).

Arnold Toynbee, *Christianity among the Religions of the World* (New York: Scribner's, 1957).

Index